Anatomy of the Ship

THE DESTROYER
CAMPBELTOWN

Anatomy
of the
Ship

THE DESTROYER
CAMPBELTOWN

Al Ross

CONWAY

MARITIME PRESS

1 Frontispiece
Buchanan at Balboa, Panama, between
1934 and 1937. By this time, the gun
platform sides had been plated in and
the pennant numbers painted correctly.
National Archives 80G1025117

© Al Ross 1990

First published in Great Britain 1990 by
Conway Maritime Press Limited
24 Bride Lane, Fleet Street
London EC4Y 8DR

British Library Cataloguing in Publication Data
Ross, Al
    The destroyer Campbeltown
    1. Great Britain. Royal Navy. Destroyers, history
    I. Title   II. Series
    623.8'254'0941

    ISBN 0–85177–543–8

Designed by Jonathan Doney
Typeset by Inforum Typesetting, Portsmouth
Printed and bound by The Bath Press, Bath

Contents

ACKNOWLEDGEMENTS

Books of this nature require exensive research, a task made much easier and far more enjoyable through the efforts of a large number of people who graciously provided assistance. To these individuals the author extends his heartfelt thanks. Among the many helping out, and in no particular order, were: A D Baker III; Chuck Haberlein; Paul Connor of the Smithsonian Institution; Dr Norman Friedman; Nathan Lipfert of the Maine Maritime Museum, who let me paw through all those marvellous tubes of plans from Bath Iron Works; Mr Willis of the Imperial War Museum; A J Francis of the Naval Historical Library; Commander John Alden, whose classic *Flush Decks and Four Pipes* will be reprinted by the Naval Institute Press by the time this work is published; Lieutenant-Commander Arnold Hague, whose book *The Towns* provides a fine overview of the careers of the 50 'flush-deckers' acquired from the USN by the RN in 1940. Without question, though, the author's greatest appreciation goes to his good friend John Lambert, who very graciously allowed him to use a large number of his excellent RN weapons drawings and generally made sure that material on the ship in RN service was made available. Readers of the Anatomy series will recognize John as the author of the volumes on HMS *Alliance* and on the Fairmile 'D' MTB/MGB, as well as a prolific writer of journal and magazine articles and a provider of intricate scale drawings of many RN ships and weapons.

ntroduction

1135 on 28 March 1942, at St Nazaire, France, the air was suddenly ttered by a thunderous explosion in the bows of an old destroyer lodged he caisson of Normandie Lock. The forward half of the ship, and a large nber of unfortunate German soldiers inspecting her, were vapourized. : caisson was breached and what remained of the old destroyer was hed into the lock by the resulting inrush of water, effectively eliminating Nazaire as a repair facility for *Tirpitz*. So ended the career of HMS npbeltown, the former USS *Buchanan* (DD 131).

MS *Campbeltown* was one of fifty obsolete flush-decked destroyers trans-ed to the Royal Navy in exchange for extended leases on a number of ish bases along the Atlantic seaboard. It was a transfer fraught with culties, despite the close ties betwen England and the United States.

n May 1940, Prime Minister Churchill made his first request for de-yers to President Roosevelt. The Royal Navy's destroyer forces were ntial to ensure the flow of materials to the island nation, but had suf-d heavy losses in the opening months of the Second World War. Al-ugh the RN had 433 destroyers in service at the end of the First World r, it began the Second with only 184 available. Despite the construction 1 new destroyers during the first year of the new war, heavy losses, icularly those associated with the evacuations of Norway and Dunkirk, brought this number down to 171. At first, Roosevelt was reluctant to ntenance the transfer. There were several reasons for this:

current sentiment in the US was isolationist;

he was up for re-election for his third term;

a law passed in 1917 made it illegal to deliver warships to a bellig-erent power;

the US Navy only had about 75 modern destroyers available, the majority of its force being the old, mass produced flush-deckers of the First World War era;

Roosevelt was concerned about agitating Hitler to the point of draw-ing the US into the war.

owing protracted negotiations, however, Roosevelt relented. Fully re that many of the old destroyers were ready for scrapping, he ap-ed to the US Congress on the basis that, since the scrap value of 50 of e vintage destroyers was only about $5000 each, the US stood to gain n naval and air bases for the extremely reasonable price of about 0,000. Despite congressional opposition, he pushed the deal through.

hortly after the transfer was approved, orders were issued for the imme-e transfer of 50 flush-deckers, from both those on active service and those in reserve. Most of the ships were in less than first-class condition. A list of defects compiled by the RN at the end of 1940 included the following:

- weak bridge structure
- unsatisfactory manoeuvring valves
- corroded superstructures
- defective hatch covers
- defective fresh water systems
- steering arrangements requiring overhaul
- many machinery defects
- leaking hulls and bulkheads
- corroded rivets in hulls
- defective torpedoes
- unsatisfactory manoeuvrability
- poor or missing ASDIC
- no radar

Despite these many problems, the 50 destroyers saw extensive service. Seven were transferred to the Royal Canadian Navy, a number were hand-ed over to the Soviet Navy, and ten were lost as a direct result of enemy action, most being sunk by U-boats.

DESIGN HISTORY

Campbeltown began life as the USS *Buchanan* (DD 131), one of 273 flush-decked destroyers built in US yards between 1917 and 1922.

The flush-deckers were designed in response to the projected need for large numbers of destroyers in a very short period of time, brought about by the advent of the First World War. Up to this point, the primary mission of the destroyer in the US Navy had been surface warfare, most recently against capital ships. The development of the submarine and its initial successes against shipping indicated a need for large numbers of hulls to meet the increased challenge. The fill this need, a design based on the previous 1000-ton destroyers (which themselves were based on the even earlier 700-ton 'flivvers') was prepared by both Bath Iron Works and Beth-lehem Steel. For purposes of mass production, the basic designs were identical, although the propulsion machinery varied among the builders to a marked degree. There were also small differences in the shape of the transom and minor fittings.

Like their earlier raised-forecastle counterparts, the new destroyers had four stacks and mounted four 4in/50 guns. Here, though, the similarities

7

TABLE 1: **SHIP'S PARTICULARS**

Class		Wickes
Length overall		314ft 4½in
Length between perpendiculars		310ft 0in
Beam		30ft 8in
Draft		9ft 1¾in
Displacement		1154 tons
Shaft horsepower		24,200 @ 430rpm
Speed		35kts
Range		3400nm @ 20kts
Armament	(USN) 1919	4 – 4in/50 Mk 12
		1 – 3in/23.5 Mk 14
		2 – 0.30 calibre machine guns
		4 – triple 21in torpedo tubes
		1 – Y-gun
		2 – depth charge tracks
	(USN) 1934	4 – 4in/50 Mk 12
		1 – 3in/23.5 Mk 14
		4 – triple 21in torpedo tubes
		2 – depth charge tracks
	(RN) 1940	3 – 4in/50 Mk 12
		1 – 12 pdr/12cwt HA/LA
		2 – 0.50 calibre machine guns
		2 – Mk V depth charge throwers
		2 – depth charge tracks
	(RN) 1942	1 – 12pdr/12cwt HA/LA
		6 – 20mm Mk 1
		2 – 0.50 calibre machine guns
Ammunition allowance – 1934		4in – 400 rounds
		3in – 400 rounds
		0.30 cal – 43,000 rounds
		0.45 cal – 6000 rounds

ended. Operational requirements necessitated a stronger hull: hence the flush-deck design. The torpedo battery was increased from four twin tubes to four triple mounts, fitted *en echelon*. Despite being marginally shorter and 200 tons heavier, the new design was rated at 35kts top speed, as opposed to 29kts for the earlier design. These enhancements can be traced primarily to an improved hull design and an additional 7000 shaft horsepower.

Although all 273 flush-deckers were built to a common design, as completed there were major differences in range, top speed, and fuel consumption that could be traced directly to the quality control efforts of the various builders. Bath-built destroyers, of which *Campbeltown* was one, had the best characteristics, while those built by Mare Island had the worst, their radius of action being just half that of the Bath ships. Unfortunately, being a small yard, Bath was able to build only twelve flush-deckers, the majority of the class being built by the various Bethlehem Steel yards. Of those transferred, the actual distribution was:

- Bath Iron Works - 7
- Bethlehem Steel - 19
- Charleston - 1
- Cramp - 3
- Mare Island - 2
- Newport News - 13
- Seattle Dry Dock - 1
- Union Iron Works - 4

SERVICE HISTORY: USS BUCHANAN (DD 131)

The USS *Buchanan* (DD 131) was the first ship to be named for Fran Buchanan, who served with distinction in both the Federal and Confe rate States navies. Admiral Buchanan was the first superintendent of US Naval Academy, commanding officer of the USS *Germantown*, USS quehana, and commandant of the Washington Navy Yard before joining Confederacy in 1861.

Buchanan was one of twelve flush-decked destroyers built by the E Iron Works between 1917 and 1920. Launched on 2 January 1919, she commissioned on 20 January 1919 and placed under the command Lieutenant H Bensen. *Buchanan*'s career in USN service was largely eventful, more than a third of it being spent in reserve in San Die California. Originally assigned to DESRON 2 at Guantanamo, Cu *Buchanan* was reassigned to DESFLOT 4 within six months and spent remainder of her first commission on the West Coast. Taken out of co mission on 7 June 1922, she spent the next eight years languishing reserve. Between her recommissioning in April 1930 and transfer to Royal Navy in 1940, *Buchanan* served with DESDIV 10 and DESDIV the Pacific, was decommissioned again between April 1937 and Septem 1939, was assigned to DESRON 32 in the Atlantic, served with the N trality Patrol and Antilles Detachment, and ended her final USN com sion patrolling the Gulf of Mexico.

On 2 September 1940, *Buchanan* arrived at the Boston Navy Yard route to Halifax, Nova Scotia. Arriving at Halifax on the 9th, she immediately decommissioned and handed over to the Royal Navy, which she was commissioned as HMS *Campbeltown*.

SERVICE HISTORY: HMS CAMPBELTOWN

Campbeltown was commissioned for service in the 1st Town Flotilla o September 1940 and sailed for Belfast. Almost immediately, her troul began. During her passage to Belfast, *Campbeltown* nearly collided v some of the other destroyers in the convoy during a storm. Several d later, while she was investigating an apparent intruder, her booster pur failed and she was left dead in the water. However, the rest of the cross appears to have been uneventful, with *Campbeltown* arriving at Belfast on September, then proceeding to Devonport on the 29th. Following a sl refit, she was assigned to the 7th Escort Group, Western Approaches Co mand, based at Liverpool. Although badly needed for patrol work, *Ca beltown* did not go into action immediately, because she had been dama in a collision at Liverpool, which put her out of the battle until March 19 During this repair period, in January, she was provisionally allocated to Royal Netherlands Navy. Some potential political problems arose when Dutch suggested renaming her *Middleburg*. Previously, all of the Town c destroyers (save HMS *Churchill*) had been named after towns sharing same name in both the US and UK. Apparently, as was the custom, so towns had already adopted their namesake ships, and the proposed ren ing was viewed as counterproductive from a public relations point of vi The outcome is clouded, as some sources state she had a Dutch crew w others indicate she did not! There also seems to have been a Polish conr tion, but again the references are vague on the details. What is clear is t she retained the name *Campbeltown* and by September 1941 she was a; under RN control.

Returning to convoy duty, *Campbeltown* was attacked several times U-boats and aircraft, but suffered no damage. On 3 August 1941, sisted *Wanderer, St Albans* and *Hydrangea* in the sinking of *U-401*. On 15 September she picked up survivors of the Norwegian motor tanker *Vinga*, which had been damaged by air attack. Her last success on convoy duty came on 25 January 1942, when she shot down a German aircraft.

Between 10 and 19 March, *Campbeltown* received her final, and most drastic, refit. During this period, she was radically altered to look like a German *Möwe* class torpedo boat. Her final mission was to commit suicide against the locks of the drydock at St Nazaire, thus denying its use as a repair facility for *Tirpitz*. At 0134hrs on the morning of 28 March, *Campbeltown*, accompanied by *MTB-74, MGB-314* and sixteen motor launches carrying commandos, rammed the lock gates. Eleven hours later, her delayed action fuses set off the 4-ton explosive charge in her bows, destroying both the ship and the lock gates.

GENERAL ARRANGEMENT AND HULL STRUCTURE

Campbeltown's hull was typical of the mass-produced, flush-decked, 1200-ton destroyers based on the Bath Iron Works designed *Wickes* (DD 75). Of all-riveted construction, the slender hull was subdivided by twelve watertight and four oil-tight bulkheads. Forward of the engineering spaces the hull incorporated a first platform deck, second platform deck, and hold, while the aft portion included only the first platform deck and hold. The engineering spaces, which comprised more than a third of the hull length, ran from main deck to keel and were arranged: boiler room/boiler room/engine room/engine room. Seven fuel oil tanks were provided, six forward and one aft of the engineering spaces. Of the six forward tanks, the first five were below the second platform deck, while the sixth extended to the first platform deck. The fuel oil tank aft of the engineering spaces extended from keel to main deck.

The hull shape was defined by a single 18in I-beam keel, to which were attached 177 frames. Seven strakes of plating were fitted on either side of the keel, varying in thickness from 0.44in (18lb) at the keel to 0.24in (10lb) at the waterline. The plating was joggled, with inner straps connecting the flush butts. From keel to sheer strake, the plates were arranged: 18lb, 15lb, 10lb, 10lb, 10lb, 10lb, 18lb. Two bilge keels, approximately 140ft long and constructed of 5in x 12in I-beam with the outer flange removed ran along either side of the hull. Above the waterline, an oak fender mounted between two steel angles provided some hull protection when docking.

Enlisted crew were accommodated on the second platform deck forward and first platform deck aft, with washroom and head located in the aft deckhouse. In USN service, enlisted accommodation was relatively spartan, although the crew slept in two- or three-tiered folding bunks. Interestingly, contemporary reports indicate that RN ratings were not overly enamoured of the bunks and preferred to sleep in their customary hammocks. As in the days of sail, the crew's quarters doubled as berthing and messing spaces. A small galley was located on the main deck between the second and third stacks, underneath the gun platform. Sanitary facilities were austere, consisting of pails for washing and a sluice for bodily functions.

Officers and CPOs fared somewhat better, sharing the first platform deck forward with the wardroom and several offices. However, officers' staterooms were smaller than those in contemporary RN destroyers and, as described by one RN officer, rather 'unhomely and austere' with their steel-framed furniture. Apparently, most of these 'defects' were remedied during Stage 1 refit at Devonport.

Superstructure on the flush-deckers was limited to a small bridge forward, an elevated gun platform abaft the bridge, and a small deckhouse aft. The bridge structure contained the chartroom, Captain's sea cabin, radio room and the bridge. A radio direction-finder and rangefinder were mounted on the roof of the bridge. As first built, the bridge was largely an open affair with canvas dodgers. During a refit early in her career, however, the bridge was plated in and a triangular deflector added below the bridge windows. The bridge structure was, unfortunately, relatively fragile and not well-suited to the North Atlantic. In 1941, HMS *Burnham* had the bridge roof crushed by a wave, jamming the helm. A similar fate befell HMS *Buxton* when a wave demolished the bridge, killing the first lieutenant, captain, and a rating.

The gun platform was built over the small galley and was initially open sided. With succeeding refits, the sides were plated in to improve habitability. A single 4in/50 was mounted outboard on either side of this platform, along with a gravity tank, ready service racks, and Carley floats. During a late refit, a practice loader was mounted athwartships behind the ready service lockers.

The aft deckhouse contained the torpedo workshop and crew's washroom. Mounted on the top of the deckhouse were an emergency steering position, Y-gun (depth charge thrower), ready service racks for the depth charges, and a searchlight platform. During her initial refit in 1923, the Y-gun, racks, and searchlight platform were removed and the aft 4in/50 was mounted in place of the Y-gun, its position being filled by the 3in/23 originally mounted forward. Later, after the transfer to the RN, the aft 4in/50 was replaced by a 12pdr HA and the 3in/23 removed altogether.

On the main deck between the gun platform and the aft deckhouse were two large engine room hatches, two large ventilators, three pairs of rather complex supports for the ship's boats, and four triple torpedo tubes mounted *en echelon*. During the 1923 refit, a tall searchlight platform was erected between the two main engine room hatches.

One of the most distinctive features of the flush-deckers (with the exception of several of the oldest) was their four tall, slender funnels. Generally, in RN service, the aft three funnels were cut down in height during the Stage 1 refit. For some reason, only the after-most funnel was cut down on *Campbeltown*, giving her a silhouette unique among her sisters.

BOILERS

Campbeltown was fitted with four Normand return flame type boilers operating at 260lb of steam pressure, with a furnace volume of 718cu ft and a heating surface of 6500sq ft.

Each boiler consisted of a large steam drum, two smaller water drums, outside downtakes and two nests of generating tubes. The shell of the steam drum was made of two lapped and riveted plates, to which the dished heads were then riveted. The shells of the two water drums were made of two welded steel plates, to which the domed heads were attached. The drums were secured in place by a brace at each end. The front end of the steam drum was supported by a hollow brace from each lower drum, each brace acting as a circulating tube.

The generating tubes were curved for the greater part of their length and entered the drums normally. The space left at the top of the boiler where the tubes met was filled with fire brick to protect the steam drum from gasses.

Each side of the furnace, for about two-thirds of its length, was formed

TABLE 2: **PARTICULARS OF SHIP'S MACHINERY**

Boilers
Type	4 Normand return flame
Steam pressure	260lb
Furnace volume	718cu ft per boiler
Heating surface	6500sq ft per boiler

Turbines
Type	2 sets Parsons with reduction gears
Steam pressure at HP turbine	240lb
Shaft horsepower	24,200 @ 430rmp

Steering engine
Type	Hyde Windlass combined hand and steam screw type, vertical engine double cylinder 6.5in × 8in
Steam pressure	200lb

Windlass
Type	Hyde Windlass vertical with gypsy head, double cylinder 5in × 4in
Steam pressure	200lb

Ventilation
Type	1 – GE 2500cu ft/m enclosed motor
	2 – GE 1000cu ft/m open motor

TABLE 3: **FUEL TANK CAPACITIES**

Tank compartment	Net capacity
A–104	22.06 tons
A–105	25.64 tons
A–106	25.64 tons
A–107	18.05 tons
A–108	18.05 tons
A–113	21.44 tons
A–114	21.50 tons
A-115	29.80 tons
D–101	34.51 tons
D–102	35.71 tons
D–103	36.02 tons

by a wall of tubes. The sides of the grate were brick walls, which protected the lower drums and the lower ends of the tubes. The two outer rows of generating tubes in each nest were bent to form a wall, while the rest were staggered.

TURBINES
Propulsion was provided by two sets of Parsons marine steam turbines developing 24,200 shaft horsepower at 430rpm. Each set consisted of two turbines (high pressure and low pressure) coupled to a reduction gear which, in turn, was coupled to a shaft. At the end of each shaft was a 110in diameter, 122in pitch, three-bladed propeller.

The low pressure (LP) unit was a composite double-flow low pressure turbine and astern turbine connected by a flexible coupling to the inboard pinion shaft of the reduction gear, while the high pressure (HP) unit was coupled to the outboard pinion shaft. Two pinions were mounted on each shaft and drove the main gear wheel. A flange on the aft end of the main gear wheel shaft bolted to a similar flange on the propeller shaft.

The flexible coupling was of the jaw type and consisted of a two-piece steel sleeve with internal teeth at each end. These teeth meshed with external teeth cut on the flanges at the after end of the turbine shaft and forward end of the pinion shaft.

STEERING
The steering engine was a combined hand and steam screw type built by the Hyde Windlass Company. A vertical, double cylinder type, the engine operated at 200psi steam pressure. The steering mechanism in the flush-deckers was archaic at best, consisting of cables running aft from the bridge to the steering engine. These cables were exposed in the machinery spaces and prone to fouling. An emergency steering position was fitted to the aft deckhouse, while a third position was fitted in the steering engine room aft. In a dire emergency, steering could be effected by a tiller mounted in a socket on the main deck between the depth charge tracks. Contemporary USN and RN reports indicate that even under ideal conditions the man-

oeuvrability of the ships was atrocious, a fact attested to by the numero collisions recorded by a variety of the Towns. (One RN report indicat that the turning circle at medium speeds was equal to that of the b tlecruiser *Hood*.) The spacing of the propellers was further criticized contributing to the steering difficulties.

GROUND TACKLE
As if to emphasize their obsolescence, the flush-deckers were fitted w two old-fashioned stocked anchors billed to depressions in the deck. T windlass, manufactured by the Hyde Windlass Company, was of the ve cal type, its double cylinders operating at 200psi steam pressure. It v fitted with a gypsy head with 1in close-link chain.

FIRE CONTROL
Buchanan's fire control equipment was very basic. As built, she carrie Dotter Directorscope and Ford Range Keeper Mk 2 on the signal platfo and a pair of torpedo directors in the bridge wings. By 1934, she carrie Bausch and Lomb 1.5m coincidence rangefinder mounted on the forwa end of the signal platform. This particular unit was criticized by the RN being inaccurate over 5000yds.

Local control was provided on each mount by a yoke sight containin telescopic sight for both the trainer and pointer. The yoke sight consisted a Y-shaped bar which pivoted in a saddle mounted on the barrel, the t telescopes, and an azimuth head mounted on a slide on the side of barrel. In operation, when a deflection setting was made on the si mount, the end of the yoke would move laterally in the azimuth head a the yoke would rotate about a vertical pivot. When the range was set, sight bar, azimuth head and end of the yoke rose together, the yoke a rocker rotating as a unit about a horizontal pivot.

SONAR
Buchanan was designed for a sonar installation from the outset, a 's marine detecting room' being shown between frames 12 and 15 on original 'as fitted' plans. Unfortunately, there is no mention of which t of listening device was carried. It would appear that an early mark of J ser (passive listening) sonar was installed. Friedman indicates that two *Buchanan*'s sisters – *Aaron Ward* (DD 132) and *Hale* (DD 133) – w fitted with type JG in 1933. Contemporary RN records, however, indic that none of the destroyers in the 1st Flotilla (of which all three of aforementioned destroyers were part) was fitted with sonar at the tim

nsfer. The standard Stage 1 refit at Devonport included the fitting of
DIC in those ships not already so fitted and *Campbeltown* was involved in
eral ASW actions during her RN service, suggesting that she may have
eed received ASDIC.

ARCHLIGHTS

her initial configuration, *Buchanan* mounted a 24in searchlight on the
dge and on a platform on the aft deckhouse. During her first refit, the aft
rchlight was moved to a tall tower between the large engine room hatches
I the forward searchlights were moved to a platform on the foremast.
h searchlights could be controlled from below or on the actual platform.
o 12in signal lights were mounted on the bridge wings, just forward of
signal flag lockers.

JN ARMAMENT

/50. The standard main armament of the flush-deck destroyers consis-
of four single 4in/50 Mk 12 mounts. As designed, *Buchanan* carried a
elded mount on the centreline forward, two wing mounts on a raised
tform between the second and third stack, and a fourth mount on the
tail (quarterdeck). Early in her career, the aft mount was moved to the
of the aft deckhouse, replacing the former searchlight platform and
un. Later, in RN service, this aft mount was replaced by a shielded
dr.

he Mk 12 mount was only intended to be used against surface targets,
maximum elevation was only 20°. It consisted of a Mk 9 gun mounted
a manually operated, cast stand. The Mk 9 gun consisted of the tube, a
in breech plug, Smith-Astbury type operating mechanism, and De-
ge gas check system. Each mount was, in turn, fitted with a yoke sight
unt containing two telescopes. The forward mount was fitted with a
ple shield.

in/23.5 Mk 14 anti-aircraft mount. The 'as designed' plans for
hanan show her fitted with two 3in/23 anti-aircraft mounts. One was
unted on the centreline between the bridge and forward 4in/50, while
ther was shown mounted to port on the main deck between the bridge
I the midships 4in/50 gun platform. However, I have been unable to find
photographic evidence that the second weapon was fitted to *Buchanan*
er sisters. The forward 3in/23 was soon moved to the fantail, replacing
aft 4in/50, which was moved up to the aft deckhouse.

he Mk 14 was a modification of the earlier Mk 13 'boat gun' and was
mmonly referred to as the Poole gun, after its manufacturer, the Poole
gineering and Machine Company. Fitted with a horizontal sliding wedge
ech, the Mk 14 fired a 13lb shell at a muzzle velocity of 1650fps (feet per
nd). Elevation limits were minus 15° to plus 65°.

2pdr/12cwt. Early in *Campbeltown*'s RN career, the 4in/50 on the deck-
se aft was replaced with a 12pdr HA/LA mount. Manually operated,
mount could be used against both surface and air targets, and thus
aced the totally inadequate 3in/23 as an anti-aircraft weapon. Like the
erican 4in/50, the 12pdr had a Welin breech plug and Smith-Astbury
operating mechanism. A rudimentary shield was fitted. During her last
, this mount was moved forward, replacing the shielded 4in mount.

0mm Mk 1. *Campbeltown* did not receive her 20mm guns until late in
career – certainly not before mid-1941. Two single Mk 1 mounts were
d in pedestal mounted, octagonal tubs arranged *en echelon* just forward
he aft deckhouse. During her final refit, four additional Mk 1 mounts

TABLE 4: **PARTICULARS OF SHIP'S GUNS**

4in/50 Mk 12

Type	Single purpose, single mount
Gun	Mk 9
Max powder pressure	17 long tons per square inch
Barrel weight	5575lb
Total weight	10,140lb to 10,470lb
Oscillating weight	7430lb to 7760lb
Recoiling weight	5800lb or 6100lb
Shield weight	736lb
Max trunnion pressure	52,000lb
Muzzle velocity	2900fps
Max range	16,200yds @ 20° elevation
Elevation limits	−15° to +20°
Ammunition weights	Projectiles
	Common – 33lb
	HC – 33lb
	Illuminating – 34.7lb
	Cartridge
	Case – 17.25lb
	Charge – nominal 14.5lb

3in/23.5 Mk 14 Mod 0

Type	Dual purpose, single mount
Gun	Mk 14
Max powder pressure	13 long tons per square inch
Muzzle velocity	1650fps
Barrel weight	593lb
Total weight	1510lb
Oscillating weight	960lb
Recoiling weight	600lb
Brake load	14,710lb
Trunnion pressure	14,750lb – horizontal
	15,340lb – 65° elevation
Elevation limits	−15° to +65°
Max altitude	16,000ft @ 65° elevation
Max range	10,100 yds @ 45° elevation
Ammunition weight	Projectiles
	AA – 12.9lb
	Common – 13.0lb
	Illuminating – 13.0lb
	Cartridge
	Case – 2.2lb
	Charge – 1.3lb nominal

12pdr/12cwt QF

Type	Dual purpose, single mount
Max powder pressure	16 tons per square inch
Muzzle velocity	2235fps
Total weight	1200lb
Elevation limits	−10° to +70°
Max altitude	19,000ft @ 70° elevation
Max range	11,750yds @ 40° elevation
Ammunition weights	Projectile – 12.94lb
	Charge – 2.75 lb

20mm Mk 1

Type	Single mount, manual
Barrel weight	150lb
Cyclic	450rpm
Muzzle velocity	2740fps
Max altitude	10,000ft @ 90° elevation
Max range	4800yds @ 35° elevation
Ammunition weights	HE
	Projectile – 0.0271lb
	Case – 0.190lb
	Charge – 27.7 grams
	APT
	Projectile – 0.0271lb
	Case – 0.190lb
	Charge – 27.7 grams
Elevation limits	−15° to +90°

were fitted on top of the midships gun platform, replacing the 4in wing mounts and the 0.50 calibre machine guns, while a further pair were mounted on the aft deckhouse.

The Mk 1 mount was essentially identical to the American Mk 4 mount. It featured a cast pedestal and a variable height cradle. The pedestal was bolted to the deck, but the pedestal head, through which the column rose, rotated about the top of the pedestal and could be locked in any position by a clamping lever. The column could be raised about 15 inches by a hand-wheel mounted on the head. Mounted on top of the column were the trunnion bracket and pivot, which also provided support for the shield, cradle spiral spring, and cradle, to which the gun was bolted. The cradle spring, mounted around the left trunnion, had one end attached to the trunnion and the other to the spring case, thus acting as a counterbalance to the weight of the gun.

The gun was a 20mm 70cal weapon consisting of four main elements:

- barrel and breech casing
- breechblock
- recoil and counter-recoil system
- trigger mechanism and locking device.

Designed for automatic firing only, the gun used some of the force developed by the explosion of the propellant to eject the empty cartridge, cock, reload, and fire the next round.

The 20mm fired fixed ammunition from a 60-round magazine at a cyclic rate of about 450rpm. In practice, an experienced crew could maintain a rate of about 300rpm. Usually, every other round or every third round in the spring-loaded magazine was a tracer.

0.50 calibre machine guns. Two single 0.50 calibre Browning machine guns were mounted on the midships gun platform, apparently during *Campbeltown*'s initial refit. The former Carley float postions on the platform were plated over and a splinter shield fitted. From the one photograph of the installation which I have seen, it appears that these were the standard USN Mk 3 anti-aircraft mounts of the period. The fact that the ships of the 3rd 'Town' Flotilla were listed as carrying 0.50 calibre Brownings on transfer, together with an allowance of 11,000 rounds per gun, seems to support this observation. I have been unable to locate any data indicating that the ship carried the 0.50s in USN service, however.

TORPEDO ARMAMENT

In USN service, *Buchanan* carried four triple 21in torpedo tubes mounted two sets per side, *en echelon*. Each mount consisted of three tubes supported by a saddle resting on the roller bearing assembly of the stand. The stand, in turn, contained a training circle. Training was done manually, the torpedoman turning a handwheel protruding between two of the tubes just forward of his seat.

Each tube assembly consisted of a main barrel, spoon, and spoon extension. The spoon and spoon extension were open on the bottom and the spoon extension was hinged at the top so that it could be folded back along the spoon to save deck space. The breech end was closed by a hinged door to form a chamber for the powder gases which expelled the torpedo from the tube. Mounted on top of the tubes were a seat for the trainer, a telescopic sight, and the mount for the training handwheel.

Within the barrel, at the bottom, were rollers which facilitated loading the torpedo. Running the length of the barrel and top of the spoon and spoon extension was a slot into which the torpedo guide stud was fitted

TABLE 5: **PARTICULARS OF THE Mk 8 TORPEDO**

Manufacturer	Bliss-Leavitt
In service	1911
Length	256.3in
Diameter	21in
Weight	2600lb
Propulsion	Turbine
Guidance	Gyro
Flask air pressure	2800psi
Warhead	466lb TNT
Exploder	Contact – Mk 3 Mod 2
Speed	36kts
Range	16,000yds

during loading. The stud prevented the torpedo from dropping downwa before the tail assembly cleared the main barrel, thus preventing damage the tail assembly and propellers.

Impulse chambers were fitted to the aft end of the barrel. These cha bers accepted the black powder charges used to launch the torpedo Normally, the charges were fired from the bridge, but could be fired loca by percussion.

During her Stage 1 refit at Devonport, the two aft sets of tubes w landed.

The Mk 8 torpedo was the standard destroyer anti-surface weapon of period. First manufactured by the Bliss-Leavitt Company in 1911, the 8 was the first USN 21in torpedo and was still in limited use at the beg ning of the Second World War. Like most torpedoes, the Mk 8 compri three main sections bolted together. The forward section contained 46 of TNT and a contact exploder Mk 3 Mod 2. The centre section contain the flask for the compressed air and alcohol fuel, while the tail secti contained the turbine, gyros and servos for the directional systems, cont rotating propellers, and the tail fins.

DEPTH CHARGES AND PROJECTORS

Buchanan was originally fitted with two release tracks at the stern an Y-gun mounted on the aft deckhouse, both of which used the new developed Mk 3 depth charge. The Y-gun was removed early in her care

The Mk 3 depth charge consisted of a sheet steel cylinder approximat 28ins in length and 18ins in diameter, a central tube containing a pist booster extender, and booster, and 300lbs of cast TNT. The pistol v adjustable and had indexed depth settings stamped on the face of carrying flange. Sink rates varied between 6 and 9 feet per second and t effective range of relative damage varied between 30ft (fatal damage) a 90ft (moderate to slight damage).

The Y-gun consisted of a cast spherical expansion chamber with t 24in by 6in smooth bore tubes set at a 45° angle. Set perpendicular these tubes was a casting housing the breech mechanism. The breech p was an interrupted-screw type, housing a firing mechanism which provic for local percussion firing by lanyard. The entire unit was fixed, no pro sions being made for training or elevation. Variations in range were tained by altering the weight of the impulse charge. Three standard weig of black powder charges were used to obtain ranges of 50, 75, and 120y

In operation, an expendable arbor (a tube with a steel tray) was fitt into each projector tube and a depth charge was chained to the arbor. Or the range had been determined and the appropriate impulse charge inser

TABLE 6: PARTICULARS OF THE Mk 3 DEPTH CHARGE

...gth	27.626in
...neter	17.625in
...ght	420lb
...rge	300lb TNT
...oder	Mk 6 – 3.5 granular TNT
...rate	6–9fps
...ctive radius of damage	30ft – fatal
	60ft – serious
	90ft – moderate to slight

...he breech, firing was accomplished by percussion ignition of the impulse ...rge in the breech, the resulting gases forcing the arbor out of the tube.

...Jpon *Campbeltown*'s transfer to the RN, the two aft sets of torpedo tubes ...e landed and a single Mk IV depth charge thrower and attendant ready ...vice racks were fitted on each side of the main deck just forward of the aft ...khouse. Manufactured by Thornycroft, these throwers could project a ...)lb depth charge between 40 and 70yds.

...ike its American counterpart, the Mk IV thrower consisted of an expan- ...n chamber, impulse chamber, and base. Unlike its American counter- ...t, the Mk IV thrower incorporated a non-expendable arbor in its tubular ...ansion chamber. An hydraulic arrestor cylinder was mounted on each ...e of the expansion chamber and attached to the arbor, thus acting as a ...bber when the impulse charge was fired. The ready service racks were ...ply braced tubes welded to the deck, onto which a single depth charge ...fitted. A davit was used to move the depth charge from the rack to the ...jector.

...IP'S BOATS

...ide variety of boats were carried by the ship during her 23-year lifespan. ...ially she was fitted with a 24ft and a 26ft motor whaleboat on the ...board side and a 21ft motor dory to port, inside which was carried a ...t punt. During her second commission, the 21ft motor dory was re- ...ced by a 24ft motor launch; however, a photo taken during this period ...shows her with a 26ft motor whaleboat in place of the 24ft motor ...nch. A 1940 photograph shows her in RN service with a single whale- ...t to starboard. The photo is not distinct enough to determine whether ...was the USN 24ft boat or the 27ft RN version.

...wo sets of tall skids constructed of lightened I-beams were provided for ...two larger boats, while the forward whaleboat simply hung from davits.

...MOUFLAGE

...oughout her USN career, *Buchanan* carried the standard light grey ...rall scheme with a 24in black boot-top and red anti-fouling below the ...erline. At least three different types of hull numbers can be seen in ...tographs:

1919 – narrow, closely-spaced, white numbers without black shading;

c1922 – broad, widely-spaced, crudely applied white numbers with- out shading;

1934 – standard, white with black shading.

...ring her refit at Devonport, *Buchanan*, now HMS *Campbeltown*, was ...ted with a Western Approaches scheme and given her new pennant ...ber, I 42. From the lightness of the colours in the few photos of her in

TABLE 7: CROSS-REFERENCE OF USN–RN NAMES AND PENNANT NUMBERS

RN name	Pennant no.	USN name	DD no.	Builder	Fate
Annapolis	I04	Mackenzie	175	Union Iron Works	RCN, declared surplus 1.4.45
Bath	I17	Hopewell	181	Newport News	Sunk by U-boat, 19.8.41
Belmont	H46	Satterlee	190	Newport News	Sunk by U-boat, 31.1.42
Beverly	H64	Branch	197	Newport News	Sunk by U-boat, 11.4.43
Bradford	H72	McLanahan	264	Bethlehem Steel	Paid off 1943
Brighton	I08	Cowell	167	Bethlehem Steel	Transferred to Soviet Navy, 1944
Broadwater	H81	Mason	191	Newport News	Sunk by U-boat, 18.10.41
Broadway	H90	Hunt	194	Newport News	In service, 1945
Burnham	H82	Aulick	258	Bethlehem Steel	Reserve, 11.44
Burwell	H94	Laub	263	Bethlehem Steel	Reserve. 1945
Buxton	H96	Edwards	265	Bethlehem Steel	Paid off, 1945
Caldwell	I20	Hale	133	Bath Iron Works	Broken up, 1944
Cameron	I05	Welles	257	Bethlehem Steel	Bombed in drydock, 5.12.40
Campbeltown	I42	Buchanan	131	Bath Iron Works	Expended as blockship, 28.3.42
Castleton	I23	Aaron Ward	136	Bath Iron Works	Reserve, 1945
Charlestown	I21	Abbot	184	Newport News	Paid off, 1945
Chelsea	I35	Crowninshield	134	Bath Iron Works	Transferred to Soviet Navy, 7.44
Chesterfield	I28	Welborn C Wood	185	Newport News	Aircraft target ship, 1943–45
Churchill	I45	Herndon	198	Newport News	Sunk by U-boat, 16.1.45
Clare	I14	Abel P Upshur	193	Newport News	Reserve, 1945
Columbia	I49	Haraden	183	Seattle Dry Dock	Paid off, 6.43
Georgetown	I40	Maddox	168	Bethlehem Steel	Transferred to Soviet Navy, 8.44
Hamilton	I24	Kalk	170	Bethlehem Steel	RCN, training duty 1953–45
Lancaster	G05	Philip	76	Bath Iron Works	Target ship
Leamington	G19	Twiggs	127	Newport News	Transferred to Soviet Navy, 1944
Leeds	G27	Conner	72	Cramp	Reserve, 1945
Lewes	G68	Conway	70	Newport News	Aircraft target ship, 1942–45
Lincoln	G42	Yarnall	143	Cramp	Transferred to Soviet Navy, 1944 stripped
Ludlow	G57	Stockton	73	Cramp	Reserve, 1945
Mansfield	G76	Evans	78	Bath Iron Works	Scrapped, 1944
Montgomery	G95	Wickes	75	Bath Iron Works	Broken up, 1945
Newark	G08	Ringgold	89	Union Iron Works	Target ship, 1945
Newmarket	G47	Robinson	88	Union Iron Works	Aircraft target ship, 1943–45
Newport	G54	Sigourney	81	Bethlehem Steel	Reserve, 1945
Niagara	I57	Thatcher	162	Bethlehem Steel	RCN, torpedo firing ship, 1944
Ramsey	G60	Meade	264	Bethlehem Steel	Aircraft target ship, 1943–45
Reading	G71	Bailey	279	Bethlehem Steel	Aircraft target ship, 1942–45
Richmond	G88	Fairfax	93	Mare Island	Transferred to Soviet Navy, 1944
Ripley	G79	Shubrick	268	Bethlehem Steel	Reserve, 1944
Rockingham	G58	Swasey	272	Bethlehem Steel	Sunk by mine, 27.9.44
Roxborough	I07	Foote	169	Bethlehem Steel	Transferred to Soviet Navy, 1944
Salisbury	I52	Claxton	140	Mare Island	Reserve, 1944
Sherwood	I80	Rodgers	254	Bethlehem Steel	Aircraft rocket target
St Albans	I15	Thomas	182	Newport News	Transferred to Soviet Navy, 1944
St Clare	I65	Williams	108	Union Iron Works	RCN, submarine depot ship
St Croix	I81	McCook	252	Bethlehem Steel	Sunk by U-boat, 20.9.43
St Francis	I93	Bancroft	251	Bethlehem Steel	RCN, declared surplus 1945
St Marys	I12	Doran	185	Newport News	Paid off, 1944
Stanley	I73	McCalla	253	Bethlehem Steel	Sunk by U-boat, 19.12.41
Wells	I95	Tillman	135	Charleston	Paid off, 1944

this pattern, it would appear that *Campbeltown* carried the white/light blue scheme, rather than the darker schemes carried by some of her sisters. One unusual feature of this particular scheme is the two small dark panels below the forward 4in mount and the depth charge projector aft. A review of the photos and text of Arnold Hague's excellent book *The Towns* suggests that these panels may have been unique to those destroyers receiving a Stage 1 refit at Devonport. Indeed, I have not found any examples of these panels on any other type of RN destroyer among the several hundred photos I have seen.

ALTERATIONS FOR THE ST NAZAIRE RAID

Between 10 and 19 March 1942, *Campbeltown* underwent a radical transformation, the intent of which was to make her resemble a German *Möwe* class torpedo boat. It was hoped that this ruse would enable her to travel the 6 miles upriver to the locks without challenge.

The forward 4in/50 mount was removed and replaced with the 12pdr from the aft deckhouse. The bridge was stripped of its deflector and sheathed with plating and splinter mattresses, while a single 0.50 calibre machine gun was mounted in each bridge wing. The stacks on the *Möwe* class torpedo boats were quite distinctive, the forward stack being about twice as wide as the after. To approximate the twin stack appearance of the *Möwe* class, *Campbeltown*'s forward stack was broadened and its top cut at an angle, the second stack was shortened and given an angled top, and both after stacks were cut down and blanked off. Four 20mm Mk 1 mounts were fitted to the midships gun platform, all boats and skids were removed, and the depth charge projectors were landed. Two 20mm mounts were mounted *en echelon* on the aft deckhouse and armour plating was fitted around the emergency conning station. The depth charge tracks were replaced with a frame for additional Carley floats. The steering wires were moved to the main deck and covered with protective plating, while two parallel rows of plating approximately 2 feet high were installed on both sides of the ship between the midships gun platform and the aft deckhouse, thus providing the commandos some measure of protection during the final assault.

SOME NOTES ON SOURCES

For readers wishing to learn more about the 1200-ton flush-deckers in both USN and RN service, the following books are excellent choices:

Admiralty, *The Town Class Destroyers*, TSD Historical Section (Bath, 1949).

Alden, John, *Flush Decks and Four Pipes*, Naval Institute Press (Annapolis, 1965).

Campbell, John, *Naval Weapons of World War Two*, Conway Maritime Press Ltd (London, 1985).

Friedman, Norman, *US Destroyers – An Illustrated Design History*, Naval Institute Press (Annapolis, 1982).

Hague, Arnold, *The Towns*, The World Ship Society (Kendal, 1988).

Mason, David, *Raid on St Nazaire*, Ballantine Books (New York, 1970).

Wingate, John, *HMS Campbeltown*, Profile Publications Ltd (Windsor, 1971).

A fairly extensive set of records on the 'Towns' is held by the Public Records Office at Kew. The National Archives in Washinton, DC, and the National Defense Headquarters in Ottawa, Ontario, hold a variety of plans for these ships. The Imperial War Museum has an extensive collection of photos of the 'Town' class (Subject List 201 – 'Town' class destroyers).

The Photographs

2 Flush-deckers in various stages of completion at New York Shipbuilding's Camden facility. The nearest ship is *Dickerson* (DD 157). *NHC*

...tern view of *Maury* (DD 100) under ...nstruction at Bethlehem Steel's Quincy, ...ssachusetts, yard. Of interest are the ...ape of the propellers, struts, and the ...oth markings. *National Archives*

4 USS *Buchanan* (DD 131) at Boston on 24 January 1919. Note the canvas dodger around the bridge and over the opening beneath the midships gun platform. *NH 50016*

5 An indistinct, but interesting photo of *Buchanan* on 26 February 1919. In comparison with the photo taken on January, the canvas dodgers have been painted grey and the numbers been applied to the hull. *NH 61469*

...ken in the early 1920s, this photo ...dicates that the bridge has now been ...closed and the deflector added to the ...idge front. The hull numbers are ...markably crude for a ship in ...mmission. *NH 69317*

7 An undated photo of *Buchanan*, but probably taken in the late 1930s. The aft 4in has been moved to the top of the aft deckhouse and the 3in/23 resited aft. *USNIP*

10, 11 Seven Bath-built destroyers
re transferred to the RN, five of them
ccessively numbered. In addition to
chanan (HMS *Campbeltown*) were:
ron Ward (DD 132) – HMS *Castleton*;
le (DD 133) – HMS *Caldwell*;
owninshield (DD 134) – HMS *Chelsea*;
d *Tillman* (DD 135) – HMS *Wells*.
NIP

9

11

HMS *Castleton* (ex-*Aaron Ward*)
...mediately upon transfer. The
...orizontal tubes against the charthouse
...e ready service racks for the 4in/50.
...M A-723

13 Secured alongside a jetty after their
arrival in Britain are HMS *Castelton* and
HMS *Clare* (ex-*Abel P Upshur*). *IWM
A–724*

14 An excellent stern view of one of the newly transferred flush-deckers. Although the censor has obliterated the first two numbers, a 3 is still visible. The cluttered appearance of the ships is evident. Note the damaged stern and missing propeller guard. *John Lambert Collection*

15 A good view of the forward 3in/23
mount. This particular ship has the
vertical ready service racks, which were
disliked by the RN. *NHC*

The primary gun armament of the flush-
deckers was the 4in/50 Mk 12 mount.
The gun appears to be at full elevation.
John Lambert Collection

17 Same view as No 16, but with a wider scope. Note the supports for the shield leading to the stand and what appears to be a commence/cease fire buzzer on the roof of the shield. *John Lambert Collection*

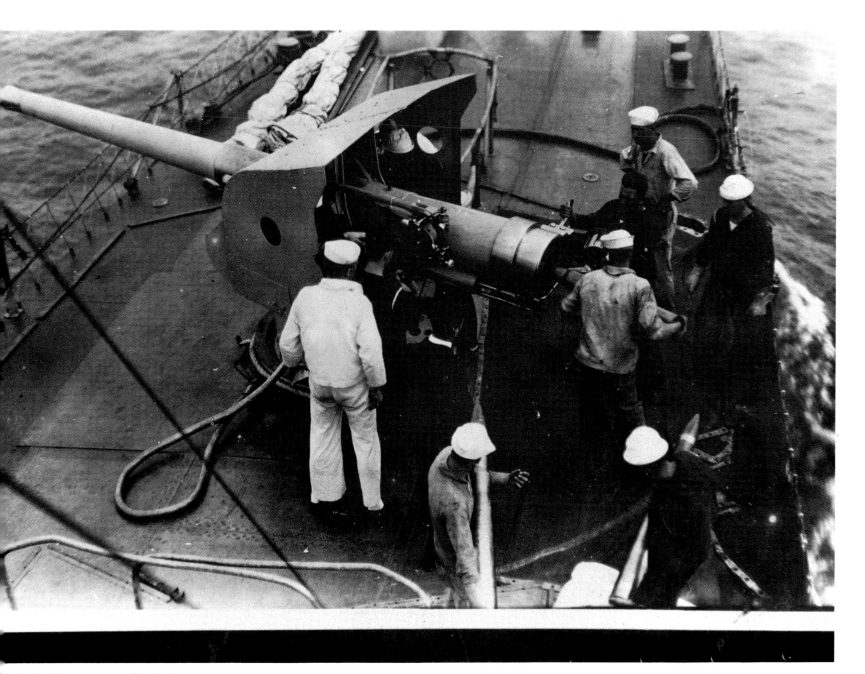

The flush-deckers were very fine-lined forward, which left little room for the gun crew. Note the size of the 4in round. *JHC*

19 The ground tackle and anchor stowa
arrangements of the flush-deckers w
quite austere, as shown in this view c
Bulmer (DD 222) taken in June 1943.
USN via Floating Drydock

21 These two photos are of several flush-deckers as converted in 1942–43 for USN service. Their value lies in the details of the torpedo tubes, engine room hatches, large ventilators, and boat skids. These are little changed from their original appearance. *USN via Floating Drydock*

21

The narrow stern left little room for depth charge tracks. The octagonal plate between the tracks allowed access to the socket for the emergency tiller. *USN via Floating Drydock*

(I)

(I)

35

23 HMS *Caldwell* (ex-*Hale*) underway in
1941. Aside from the new paint, she is
little altered, although the aft sets of
tubes appear to have been landed.
Note the dark panels below the forward
gun mount and just forward of the aft
deckhouse. *IWM A–1445*

HMS *Castleton* (ex-*Aaron Ward*) in
1942, much modified from her original
configuration. The bridge has been
rebuilt, Type 271 radar added, and
(apparently) the wing 4in replaced with
a single 20mm. *IWM A–1451*

25 HMS *Campbeltown* under refit prior to
the St Nazaire raid. The bridge has
been stripped, armoured, and has some
of the splinter matting in place. The
forward 4in has been replaced with a
12 pdr. *IWM HU53259*

Campbeltown's aft 20mm bandstands during the pre-raid refit in March 1942. The bulkheads behind which the commandos were to lie have been ...ted. *IWM HU53252*

27 The well-known view of *Campbeltown* wedged in the locks at St Nazaire, just prior to exploding. *IWM HU2242*

The Drawings

order to make the best use of the page size the drawings have been
roduced to the scale of 1/256 ($\frac{3}{64}$ of an inch = 1 foot), with large scale
wings usually in multiples of that – 1/128, 1/64 and 1/32 (respectively
, $\frac{3}{16}$ and $\frac{3}{8}$ of an inch = 1 foot).

A General arrangements

A1   **OUTBOARD PROFILE USS
BUCHANAN (DD 131) as designed,
1919 (all drawings in this section
1/256 scale, except where
otherwise marked)**

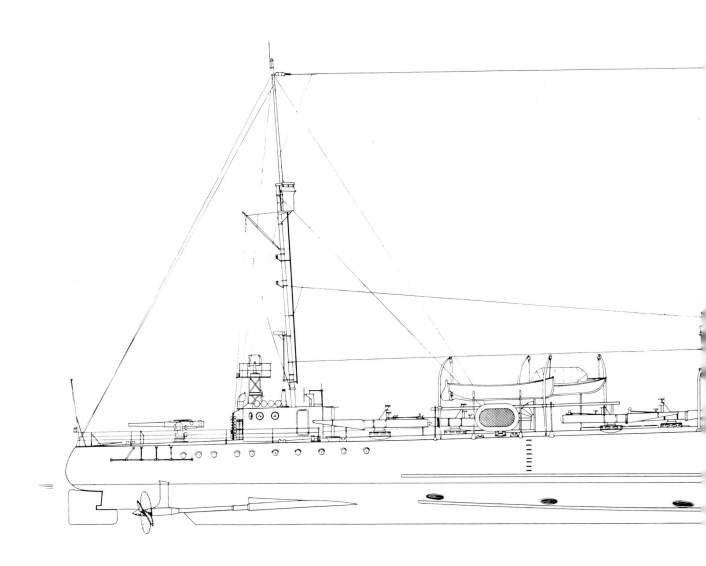

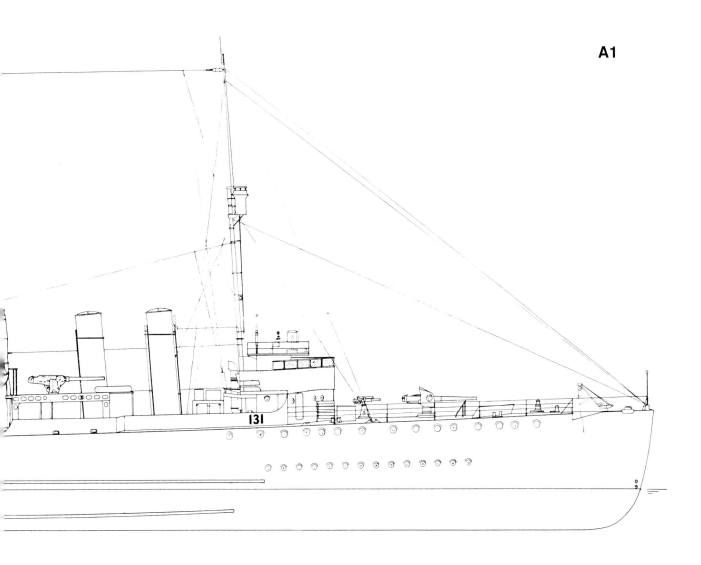

A1

A General arrangements

A2 OUTBOARD PROFILE USS
BUCHANAN (DD 131) as in 1940,
just before transfer to the RN

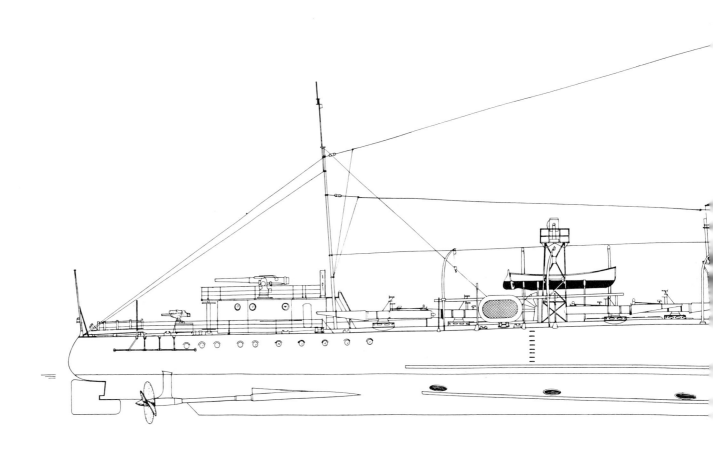

A2

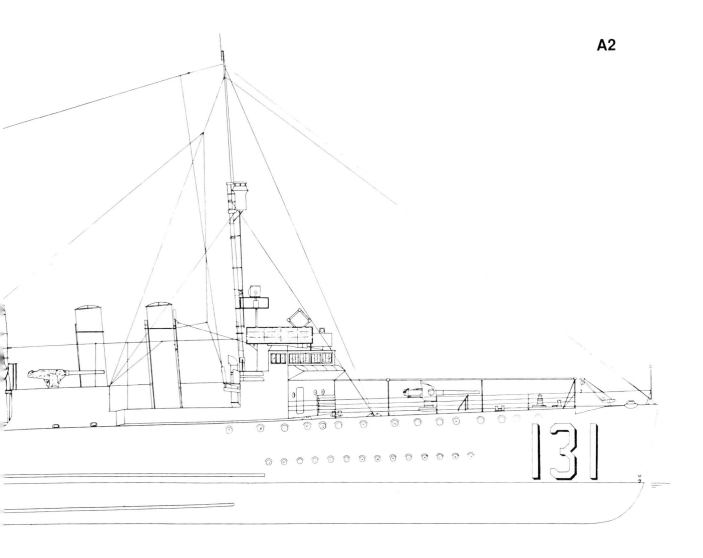

131

A General arrangements

A3 **OUTBOARD PROFILE HMS CAMPBELTOWN** upon completion of Stage 1 refit, 1941

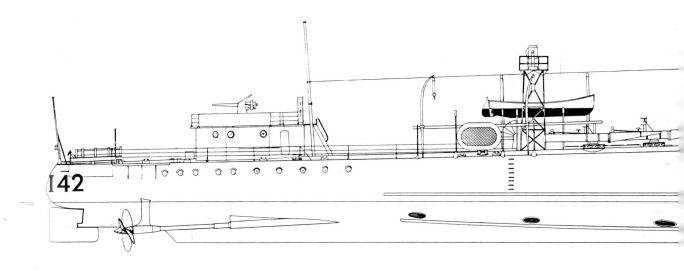

A3

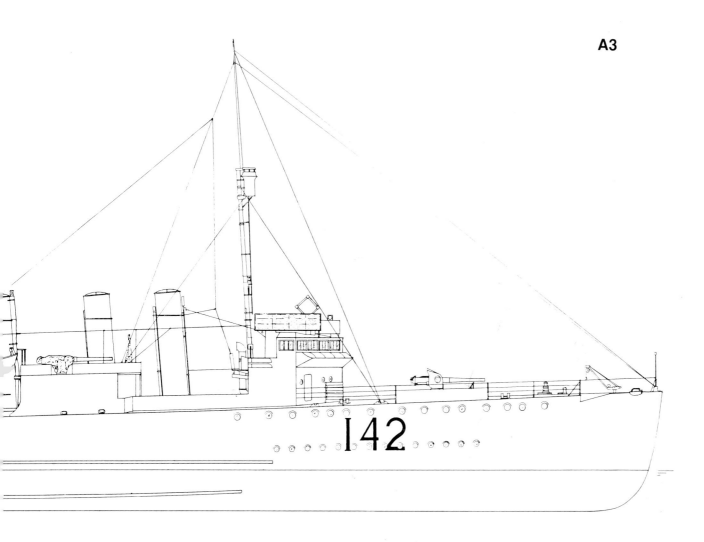

142

A General arrnagements

A4 **OUTBOARD PROFILE HMS CAMPBELTOWN as configured for the St Nazaire raid, March 1941. This particular view is based primarily on a series of photos taken during her 10–19 March 1942 refit, so is somewhat conjectural**

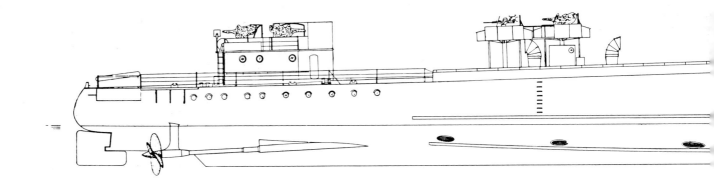

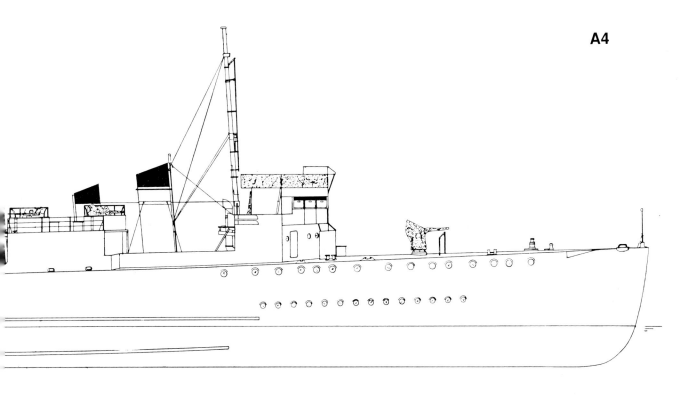

A4

A General arrangements

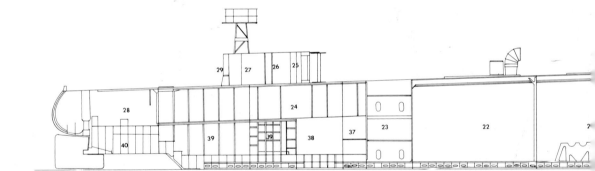

A5

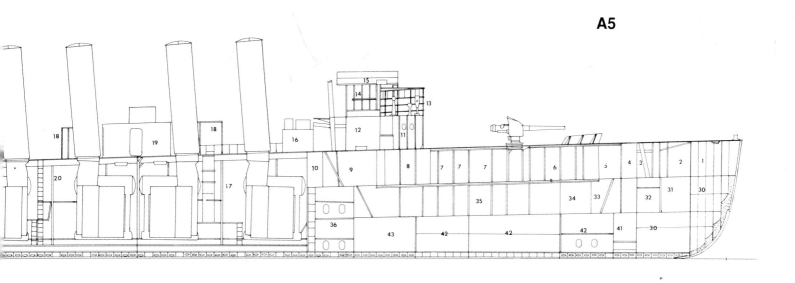

A General arrangements

A6 **MAIN DECK LEVEL as designed, 1919**

1 Bow chock
2 Closed chock
3 Anchor davit
4 Anchor bill
5 Raised water-tight hatch
6 Chain pipes
7 Capstan
8 Hatch to first platform deck
9 Open chock
10 Bitt
11 Breakwater
12 Depression rail
13 4in/50 mount
14 3in/23 mount
15 3in ready service lockers
16 4in ready service racks
17 Chartroom
18 Radio room
19 Blower
20 Raised water-tight hatches
21 Refrigerator
22 Sounding machine
23 Raised water-tight hatch to forward boiler room
24 Inflammables locker
25 Collision mat locker
26 Vegetable locker
27 Galley
28 Vents
29 Workbench
30 Breadbox
31 Lifejacket locker
32 Torpedo tube base
33 Forward engine room hatch
34 Aft engine room hatch
35 Engine room vent
36 Boat davits
37 Hawse reel
38 Torpedo workshop
39 Crew's washroom
40 Crew's head
41 Accommodation ladder
42 Propeller guard
43 Emergency tiller socket
44 Stern chock

A7 **AFT DECKHOUSE as designed 1919**

1 After steering
2 Compass house
3 Vent
4 Searchlight platform
5 Vent
6 Y-gun

A8 **MIDSHIPS GUN PLATFORM as designed, 1919**

1 Carley float
2 4in/50 mount
3 Gravity tank
4 Ready service racks

A9 **BRIDGE as designed, 1919**

1 Steering stand
2 Gyro repeater
3 Pelorus
4 Torpedo director, port and starbo
5 Signal flag lockers
6 Rangefinder
7 Dotter Directorscope
8 24in searchlight

A7

A6

A8

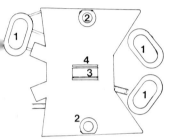

A9

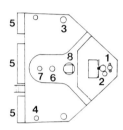

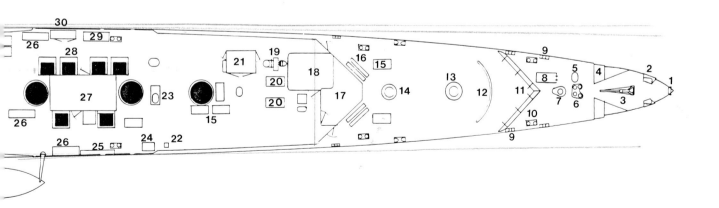

A General arrangements

A10 MAIN DECK LEVEL as in 1940

1 Bow chock
2 Closed chock
3 Anchor davit
4 Anchor bill
5 Raised water-tight hatch
6 Chain pipes
7 Capstan
8 Hatch to first platform deck
9 Open chock
10 Bitt
11 Breakwater
12 Depression rail
13 4in/50 mount
14 4in ready service racks
15 Radio room
16 Chartroom
17 Blower
18 Raised water-tight hatches
19 Raised water-tight hatch to forward
   boiler room
20 Sounding machine
21 Inflammables locker
22 Galley
23 Vents
24 Workbench
25 Breadbox
26 Collison mat locker
27 Refrigerator
28 Breadbox
29 Torpedo tube base
30 Forward engine room hatch
31 Searchlight platform base
32 Engine room vent
33 Aft engine room hatch
34 Torpedo workshop
35 Crew's washroom
36 Crew's head
37 Hawse reel
38 3in/23 mount
39 3in ready service locker
40 Propeller guard
41 Depth charge tracks
42 Emergency tiller socket
43 24ft motor whaleboat

A11 AFT DECKHOUSE as in 1940

1 Ladder
2 Compass house
3 After steering
4 Vent
5 4in/50 mount
6 Vent

A12 MIDSHIPS GUN PLATFORM as 1940

1 Ladder
2 4in/50 mount
3 Portable plate
4 Gravity tank
5 4in practice loader
6 4in ready service racks

A13 BRIDGE as in 1940

1 Helm
2 Chart table
3 Chair
4 Pelorus
5 Torpedo director
6 Vent
7 Signal flag lockers

A14 SIGNAL PLATFORM as in 194

1 Rangefinder box
2 Rangefinder
3 Direction-finder
4 Directorscope
5 Railing
6 24in searchlight
7 Vertical ladder

A11

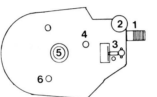

A10

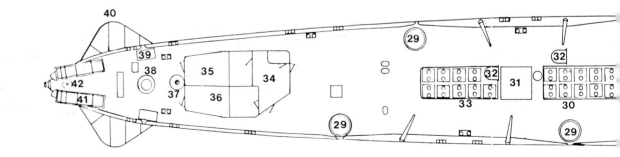

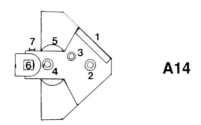

A14

A12

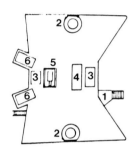

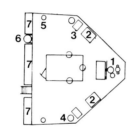

A13

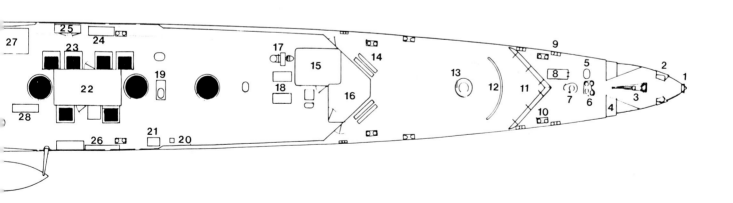

A General arrangements

A15 MAIN DECK LEVEL as in 1941

1 Bow chock
2 Closed chock
3 Anchor davit
4 Anchor bill
5 Raised water-tight hatch
6 Chain pipes
7 Capstan
8 Hatch to first platform deck
9 Open chock
10 Bitt
11 Depression rail
12 4in/50 mount
13 4in ready service racks
14 Chartroom
15 Radio room
16 Blower
17 Raised water-tight hatches
18 Raised water-tight hatch to forward boiler room
19 Raised water-tight hatch
20 Sounding machine
21 Inflammables locker
22 Galley
23 Vents
24 Workbench
25 Breadbox
26 Collision mat locker
27 Refrigerator
28 Breadbox
29 Torpedo tube base
30 Forward engine room hatch
31 Searchlight platform base
32 Engine room vent
33 Aft engine room hatch
34 Torpedo workshop
35 Crew's washroom
36 Crew's head
37 Hawse reel
38 Depth charge tracks
39 Sponson for depth charge tracks
40 Propeller guards
41 Emergency tiller socket
42 Depth charge projector

A16 AFT DECKHOUSE as in 1941

1 Ladder
2 Compass house
3 After steering
4 Vent
5 12pdr/12cwt mount
6 Vent

A17 MIDSHIPS GUN PLATFORM as 1941

1 0.50 calibre machine gun
2 4in/50 mount
3 Portable plate
4 Gravity tank
5 4in practice loader
6 4in ready service racks

A18 BRIDGE as in 1941

1 Helm
2 Chart table
3 Chair
4 Pelorus
5 Torpedo director
6 Vent
7 Signal flag lockers

A19 SIGNAL PLATFORM as in 1941

1 Rangefinder box
2 Rangefinder
3 Direction-finder
4 Directorscope
5 Railing
6 Vertical ladder

A16

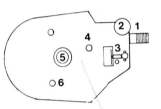

A15

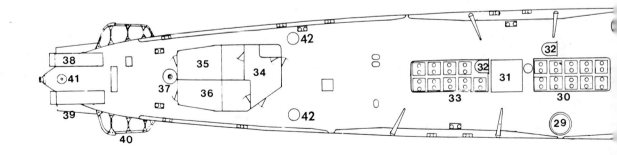

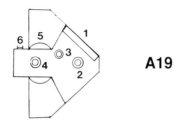

A19

A17

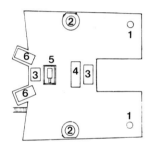

A18

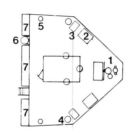

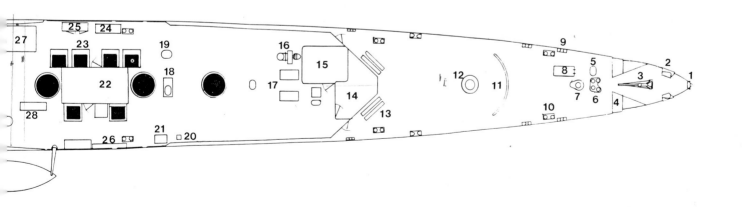

A General arrangements

A20   MAIN DECK LEVEL as in 1942

1   Bow chock
2   Closed chock
3   Anchor bill
4   Raised water-tight hatch
5   Chainpipes
6   Capstan
7   Hatch to first platform deck
8   Depression rail
9   12pdr/12cwt
10 12pdr ready service lockers
11 Radio room
12 Chartroom
13 Raised water-tight hatches
14 Blower
15 Raised water-tight hatch to forward
    boiler room
16 Galley
17 Vents
18 Capped No 3 stack
19 Capped No 4 stack
20 Forward engine room hatch
21 Engine room vent
22 Temporary sickbay
23 Aft engine room vent
24 Aft engine room hatch
25 Armoured fences
26 Hatch
27 20mm bandstand pedestal
28 Torpedo repair workshop
29 Crew's washroom
30 Scuttle
31 Sponson for depth charge tracks
32 Propeller guard

A21   AFT DECKHOUSE as in 1942

1   20mm gun tub
2   After steering
3   Compass house
4   20mm ready service lockers
5   Hawse reel
6   Vertical ladder

**A22   MIDSHIPS GUN PLATFORM as
1942**

1   20mm gun tub
2   20mm ready service lockers
3   Speaking tube
4   Vent
5   Locker

A23   BRIDGE as in 1942

1   Helm
2   Chart table
3   0.50 calibre machine gun
4   Signal flag locker
5   Sea cabin
6   Pelorus

A24   SIGNAL PLATFORM as in 194

A21

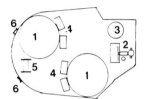

A20

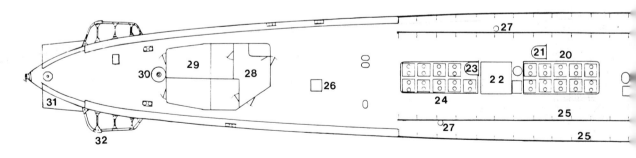

58

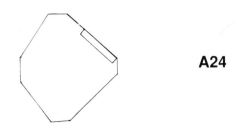

A24

A22

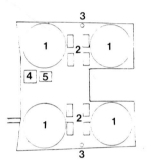

A23

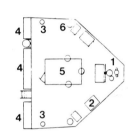

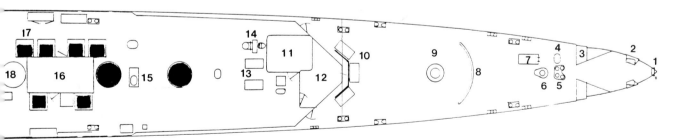

A General arrangements

A25   HOLD as in 1919

1   Peak tank
2   Listening room (ASDIC)
3   Fuel oil tanks
4   Small arms stores
5   Passage
6   4in ammunition
7   Forward boiler room
8   Aft boiler room
9   Forward engine room
10   Aft engine room
11   Handling room
12   4in ammunition
13   Stores
14   Peak tank

A26   FIRST PLATFORM DECK as in 1919

A26/1 Aft

1   Fuel oil tanks
2   Crew's quarters
3   Steering gear room

A26/2 Forward

1   Lamproom
2   Storeroom
3   Crew's washroom
4   CPO's quarters
5   Wardroom and officers' stateroom
6   Pantry
7   Yeoman's office
8   Passage
9   Captain's stateroom
10   Officers' stateroom

A27   SECOND PLATFORM DECK as 1919

1   Peak tank
2   Paint locker
3   Chain locker
4   Electrical stores
5   Medical stores
6   Ordnance stores
7   Crew quarters
8   Fuel oil tanks

A26/1

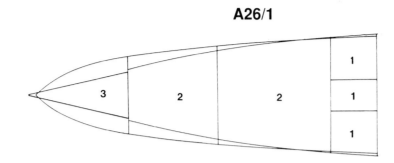

A25

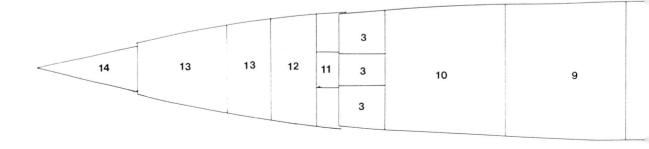

A26/2

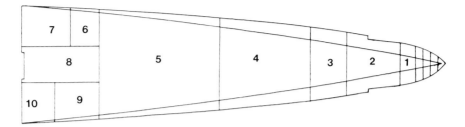

A27

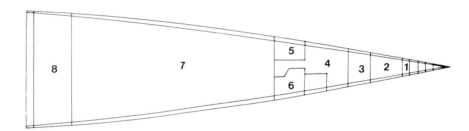

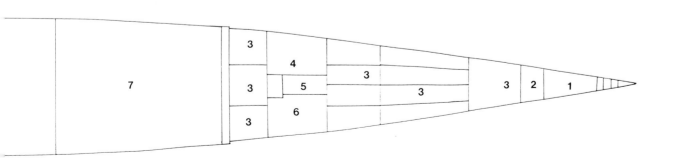

A General arrangements

A28

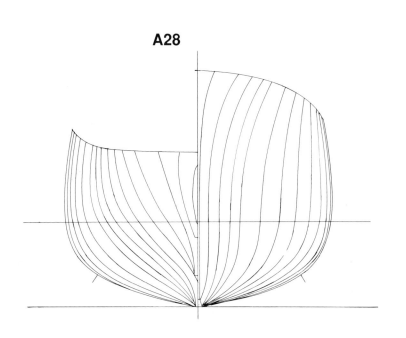

A29

A30

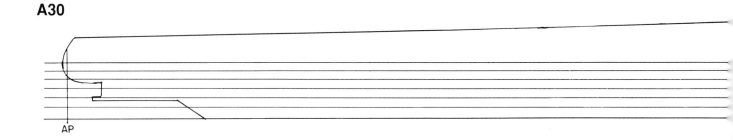

AP

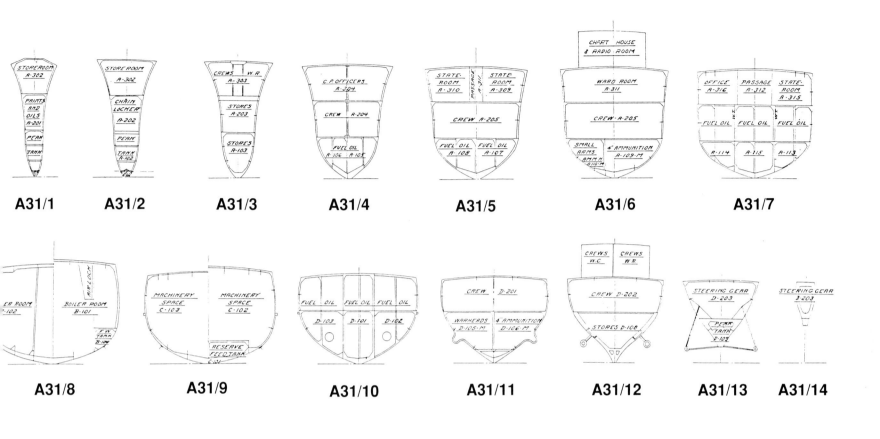

A31/1 **A31/2** **A31/3** **A31/4** **A31/5** **A31/6** **A31/7**

A31/8 **A31/9** **A31/10** **A31/11** **A31/12** **A31/13** **A31/14**

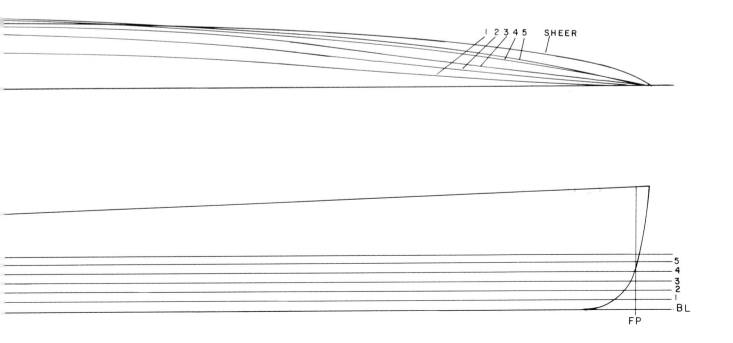

A General arrangements

A32   FORWARD SECTION as in 1919
(Drawings A44 to A55 divide the
ship in approximate thirds and
allow comparisons of the
alterations to each portion; all are
1/192 scale)

1	Bow chock	11	3in/23
2	Jackstaff	12	3in ready service locker
3	Closed chock	13	4in ready sevice racks
4	Anchor davit	14	Canvas dodger
5	Bollard	15	24in searchlight
6	Capstan	16	Rangefinder
7	Breakwater	17	Dotter Directorscope
8	Bitts	18	Vent
9	Depression rail	19	Refrigerator
10	4in/50	20	Whistle
		21	Ladder
		22	Awning rail
		23	Antenna trunk
		24	Signal flag locker
		25	Radio direction finder loop
		26	Deflector
		27	12in signal lamp
		28	12pdr/12cwt
		29	Shield
		30	12pdr ready service locker
		31	0.50 calibre Mk 3 mount
		32	Modified forward stack

A32

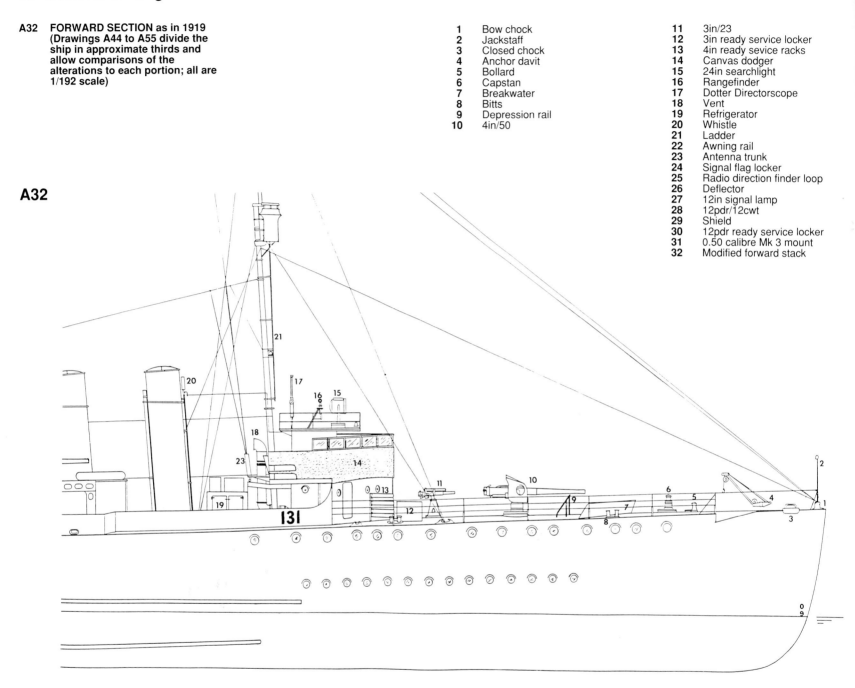

3

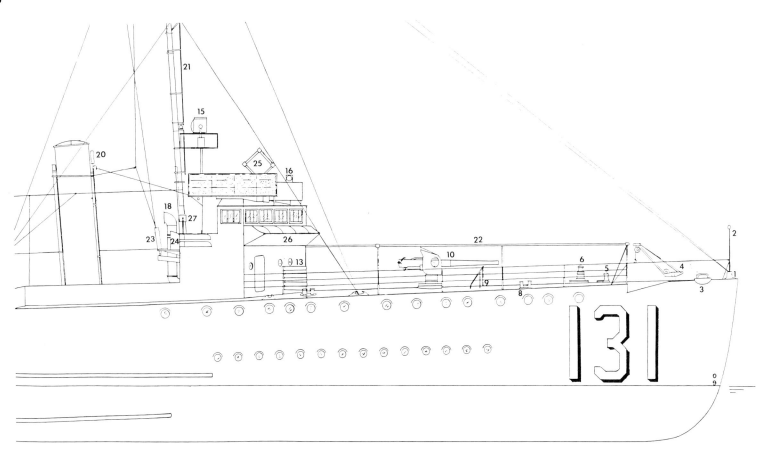

A General arrangements

A34 FORWARD SECTION as in 1941

1   Bow chock
2   Jackstaff
3   Closed chock
4   Anchor davit
5   Bollard
6   Capstan
7   Breakwater
8   Bitts
9   Depression rail
10 4in/50

11 3in/23
12 3in ready service locker
13 4in ready sevice racks
14 Canvas dodger
15 24in searchlight
16 Rangefinder
17 Dotter Directorscope
18 Vent
19 Refrigerator
20 Whistle
21 Ladder
22 Awning rail
23 Antenna trunk
24 Signal flag locker
25 Radio direction finder loop
26 Deflector
27 12in signal lamp
28 12pdr/12cwt
29 Shield
30 12pdr ready service locker
31 0.50 calibre Mk 3 mount
32 Modified forward stack

A34

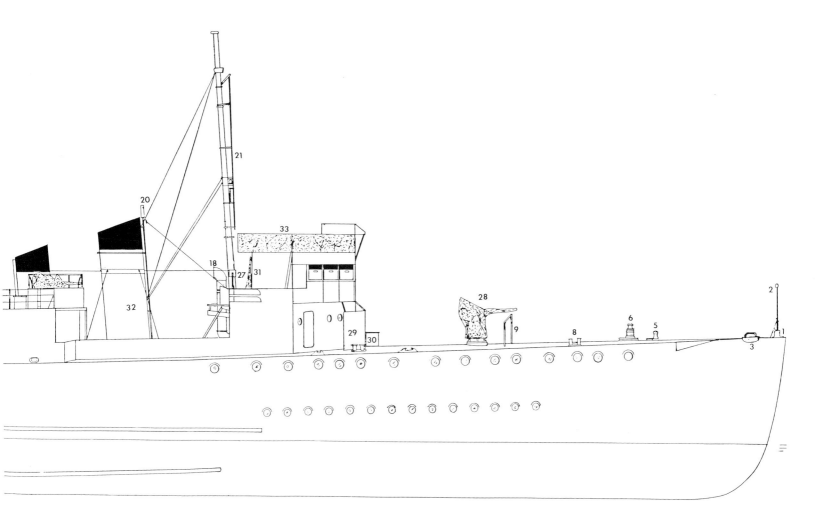

A General arrangements

A36 MIDSHIPS SECTION as in 1919

1	Carley float	21	Depression rail for 20mm
2	Wing 4in/50	22	20mm tube
3	Galley	23	Lowered No 3 stack
4	4in ready service racks	24	Locker
5	Galley smoke pipe	25	Lowered No 4 stack
6	24ft whaleboat	26	Armour fences
7	Carley float support	27	Temporary sickbay
8	Hatch to forward boiler room	28	20mm Mk 1
9	Triple torpedo tube	29	20mm ready service locker
10	Forward engine room hatch		
11	21ft motor dory		
12	Engine room vent		
13	Boat davit		
14	26ft motor launch		
15	Searchlight platform		
16	24in searchlight		
17	27ft motor whaleboat		
18	Shield		
19	0.50 calibre machine gun		
20	Modified forward stack		

A36

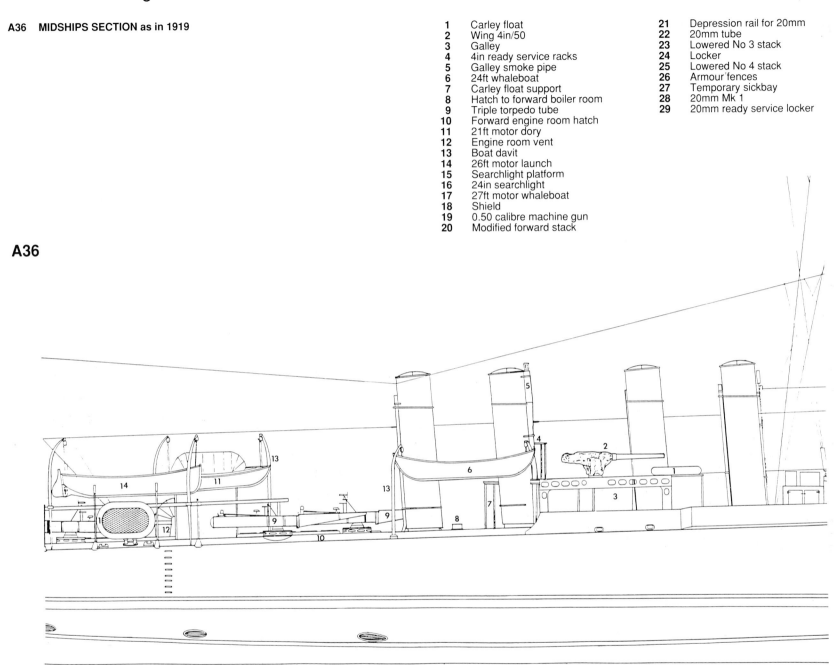

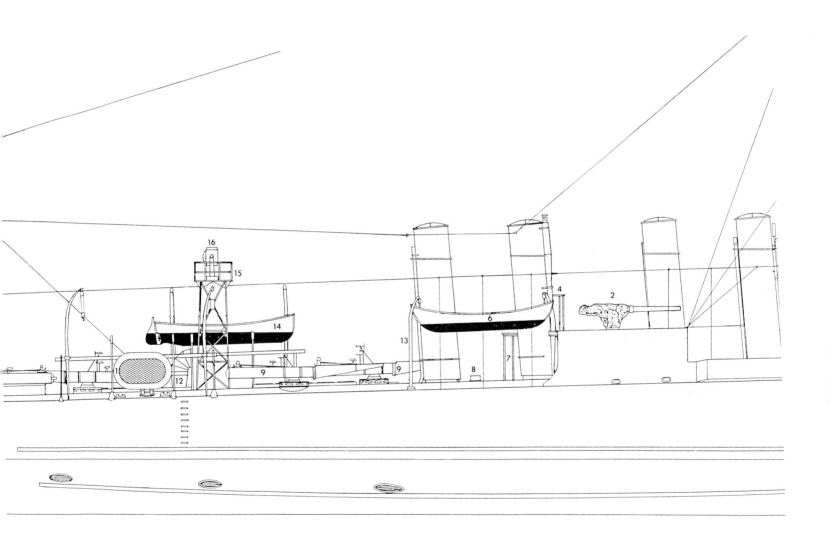

A General arrangements

A38 MIDSHIPS SECTION as in 1941

1 Carley float
2 Wing 4in/50
3 Galley
4 4in ready service racks
5 Galley smoke pipe
6 24ft whaleboat
7 Carley float support
8 Hatch to forward boiler room
9 Triple torpedo tube
10 Forward engine room hatch
11 21ft motor dory
12 Engine room vent
13 Boat davit
14 26ft motor launch
15 Searchlight platform
16 24in searchlight
17 27ft motor whaleboat
18 Shield
19 0.50 calibre machine gun
20 Modified forward stack

21 Depression rail for 20mm
22 20mm tube
23 Lowered No 3 stack
24 Locker
25 Lowered No 4 stack
26 Armour fences
27 Temporary sickbay
28 20mm Mk 1
29 20mm ready service locker

A38

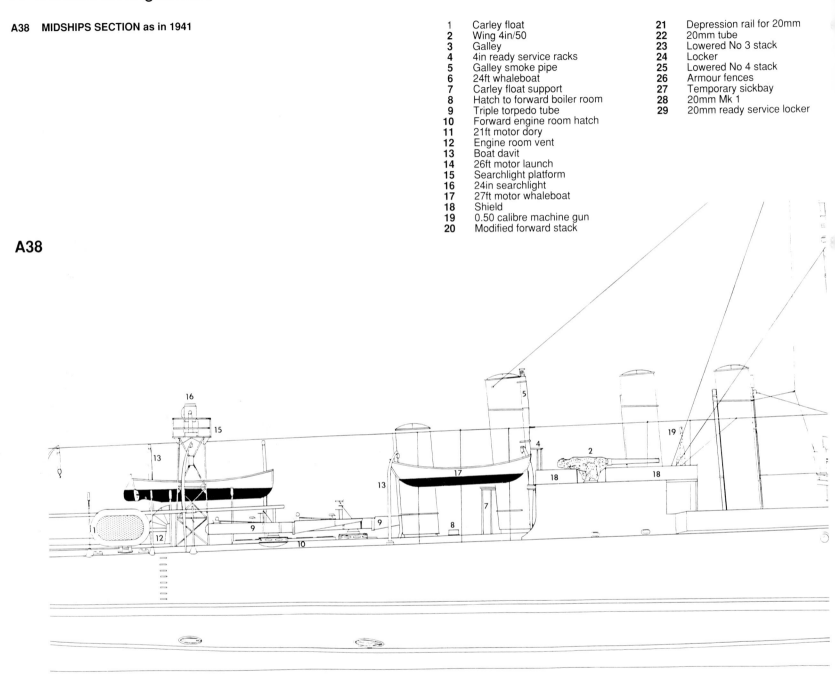

39

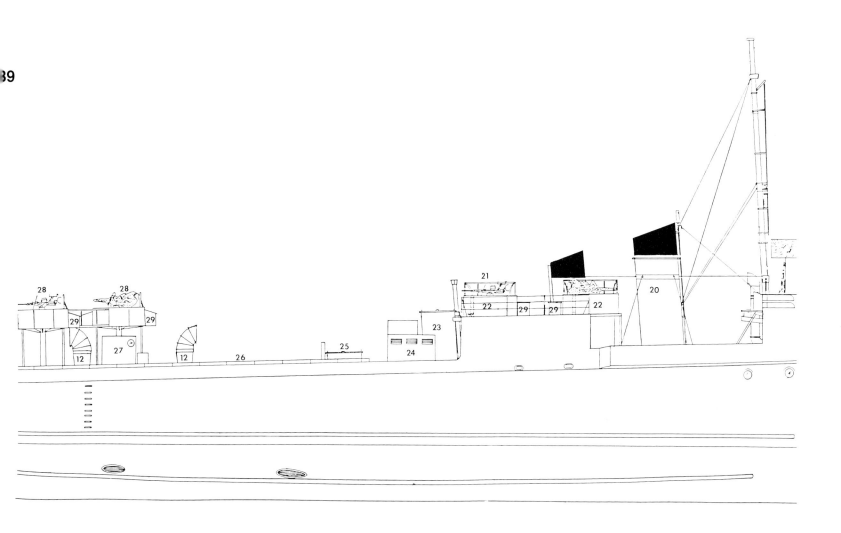

A General arrangements

A40   AFT SECTION as in 1919

1	21ft motor dory
2	24ft motor launch
3	Carley float
4	Engine room vent
5	Boat davit
6	21in triple torpedo tube
7	Hawse reel
8	After steering
9	Y-gun
10	Depth charge ready service

11	Searchlight platform
12	24in searchlight
13	4in ready service racks
14	4in/50
15	Depression rail
16	Emergency tiller
17	Sternchock
18	Propeller guard
19	3in/23
20	Hawse reel
21	Depth charge tracks
22	Ladder
23	Searchlight platform
24	24in searchlight
25	12pdr/12cwt
26	Shield
27	12in signal lamp
28	Hawse reel
29	Ladder, port and starboard
30	Carley floats
31	20mm Mk 1
32	Armour around after steering
33	Armour fences
34	Sponson for depth charge tracks

A40

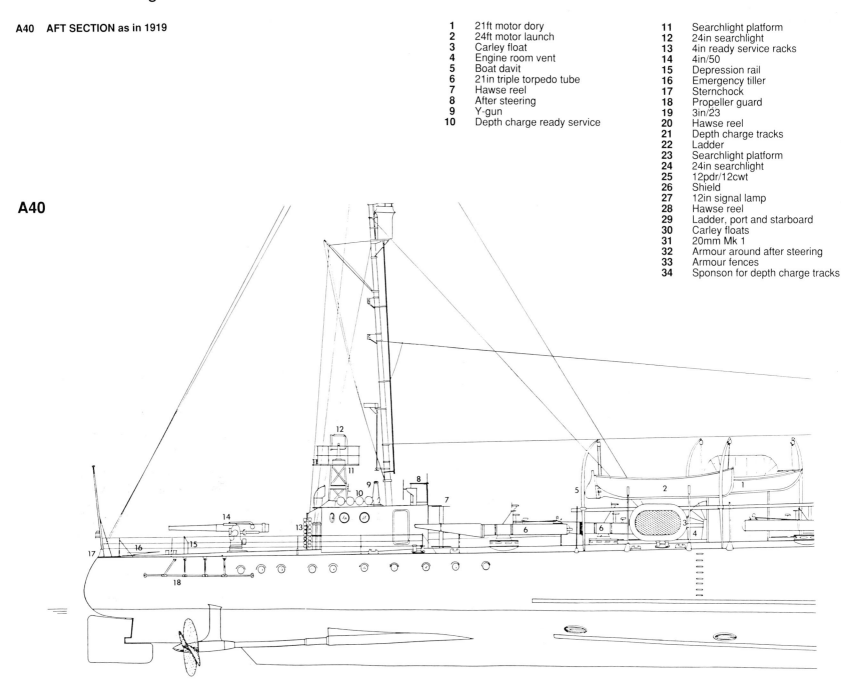

1

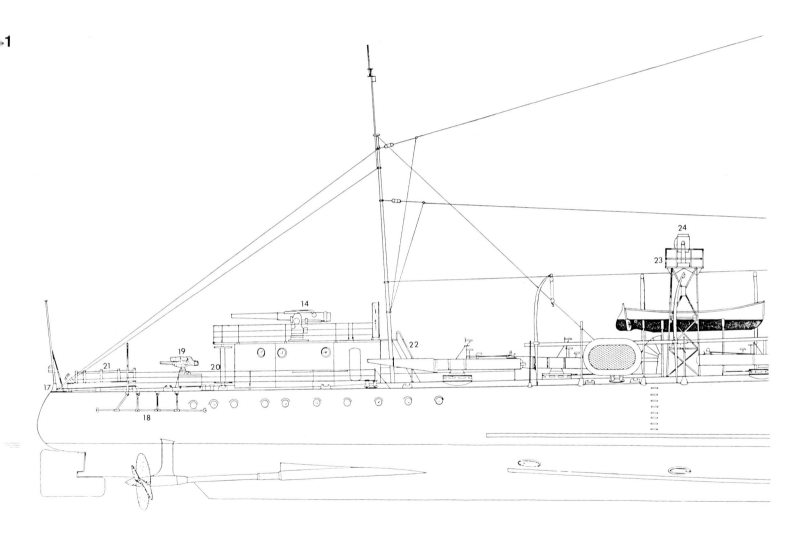

A General arrangements

A42   AFT SECTION as in 1941

1	21ft motor dory
2	24ft motor launch
3	Carley float
4	Engine room vent
5	Boat davit
6	21in triple torpedo tube
7	Hawse reel
8	After steering
9	Y-gun
10	Depth charge ready service
11	Searchlight platform
12	24in searchlight
13	4in ready service racks
14	4in/50
15	Depression rail
16	Emergency tiller
17	Sternchock
18	Propeller guard
19	3in/23
20	Hawse reel

21	Depth charge tracks
22	Ladder
23	Searchlight platform
24	24in searchlight
25	12pdr/12cwt
26	Shield
27	12in signal lamp
28	Hawse reel
29	Ladder, port and starboard
30	Carley floats
31	20mm Mk 1
32	Armour around after steering
33	Armour fences
34	Sponson for depth charge tracks

A42

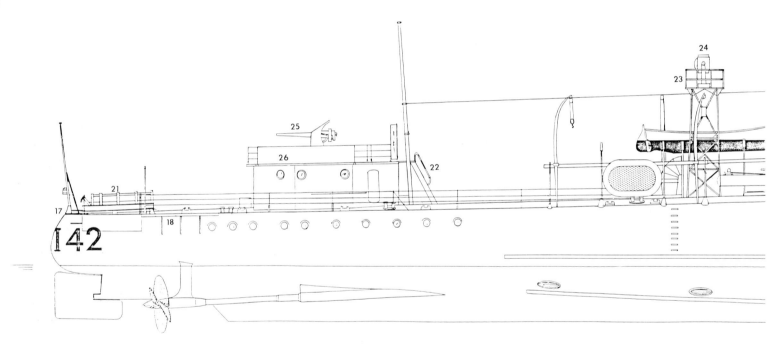

43

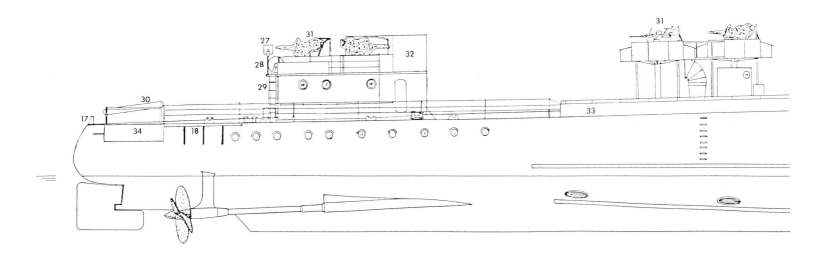

B Hull construction

B1 FRAME 88/89 looking forward, as designed (from original plans; 1/64 scale)

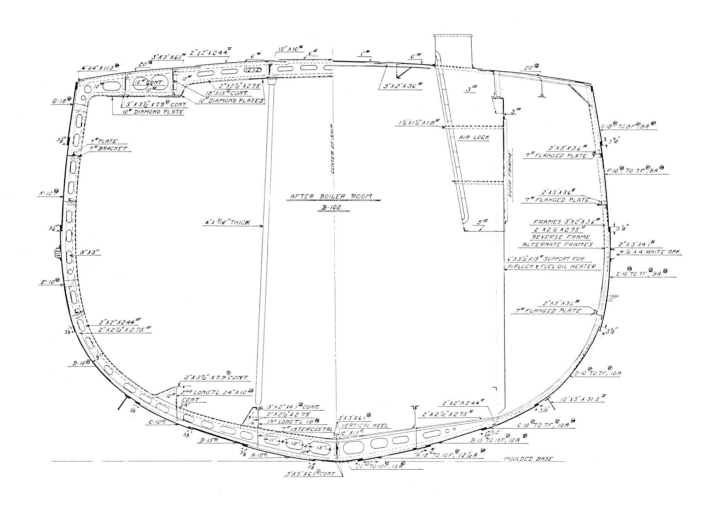

B1

**FRAME 88 looking forward/89
looking aft, as built (from original
plans; 1/64 scale)**

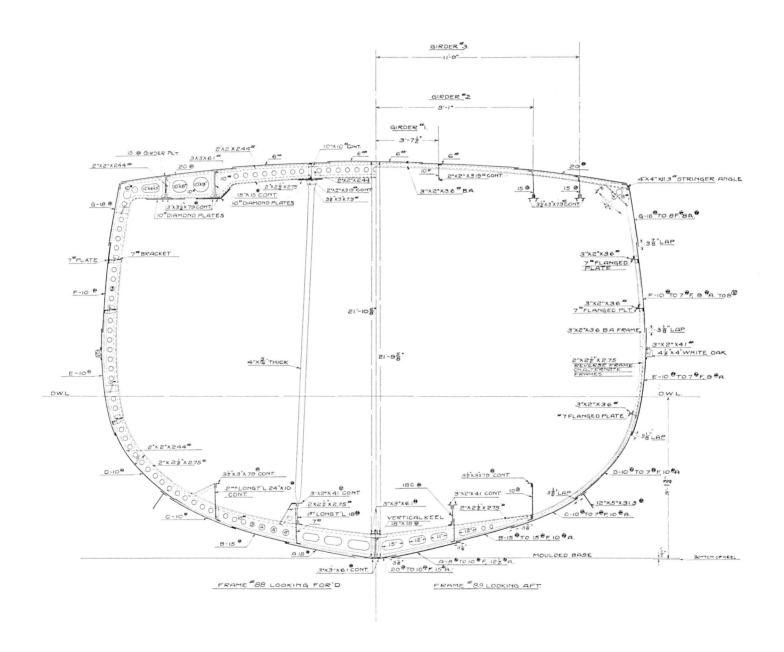

B Hull construction

B3   **PLATING EXPANSION**

1   20lb plate
2   18lb plate
3   15lb plate
4   10lb plate

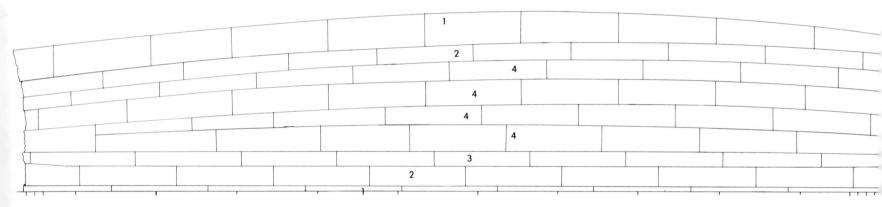

B3

PROPELLER GUARDS

As fitted in USN service (1/64 scale)

B4/1

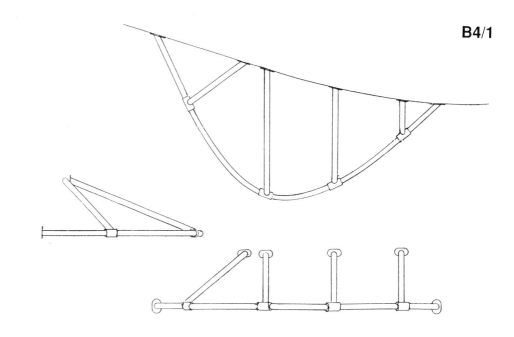

As fitted in RN service (1/64 scale)

B4/2

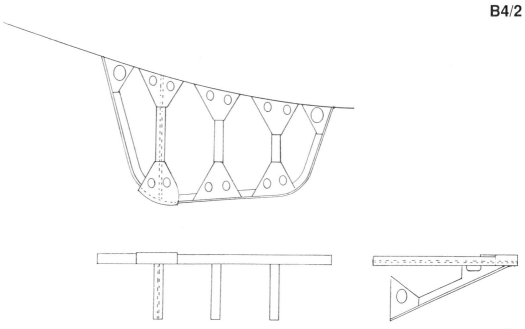

C1

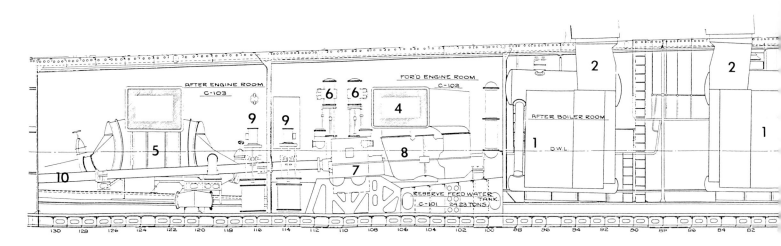

C2

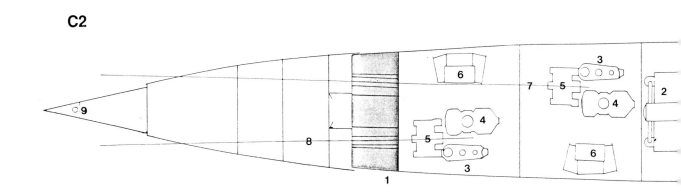

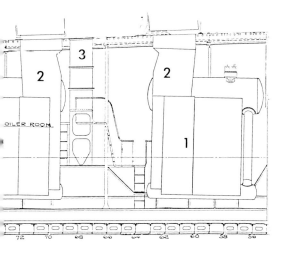

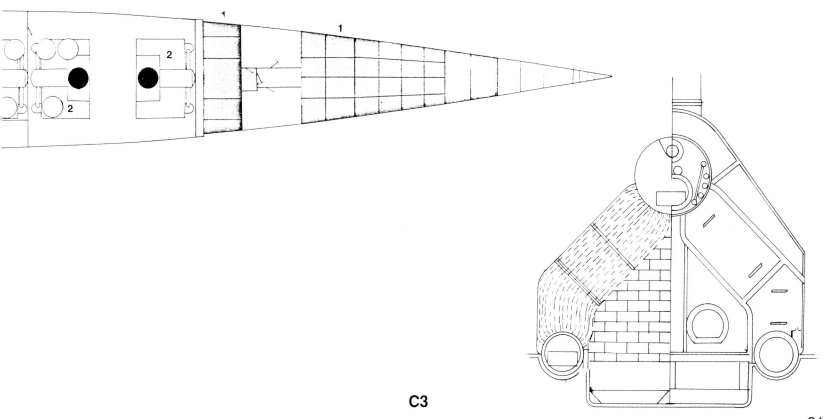

C3

C Machinery

C4   **CONDENSER** (no scale)

C4/1   Section

C4/2   Side view

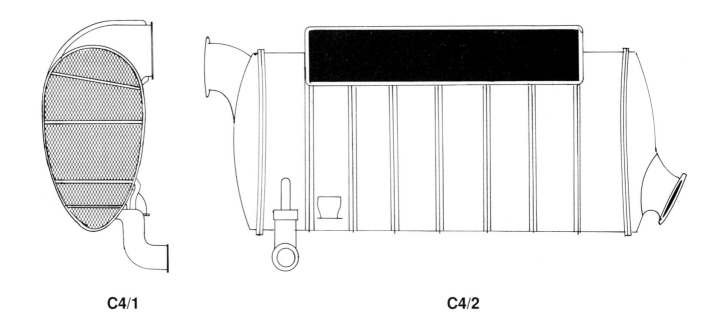

C4/1   **C4/2**

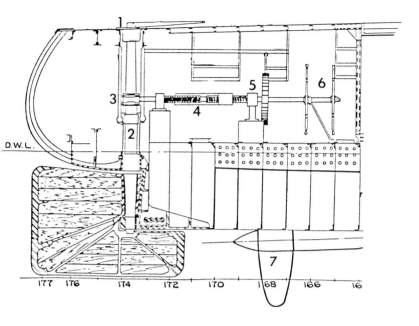

C5 **STEERING GEAR (no scale)**

1 Emergency tiller
2 Rudder stock
3 Tiller
4 Steering screw
5 Screw strut
6 Double helm
7 Port propeller

C6 **PROPELLER SHAFT (1/96 scale)**

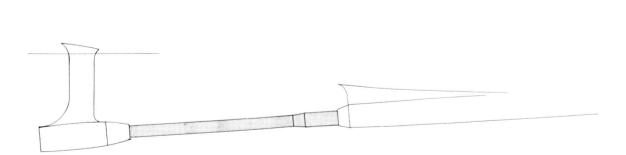

D Accommodation

D1/1

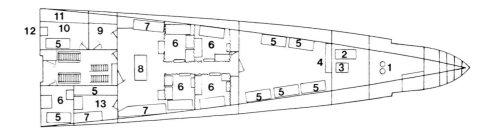

D1/2

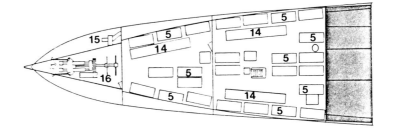

1 Chain pipes
2 Hatchway
3 Hatch
4 Locker
5 Berth (double or triple in crew's quarters, single in officers' staterooms)
6 Officer's stateroom
7 Transom
8 Wardroom table
9 Pantry
10 Yeoman's office
11 Desk
12 Locker
13 CO's cabin
14 Mess table
15 1000cu ft/min fresh air blower
16 Steering gear

D2

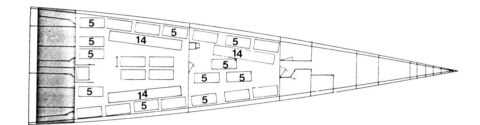

E Superstructure

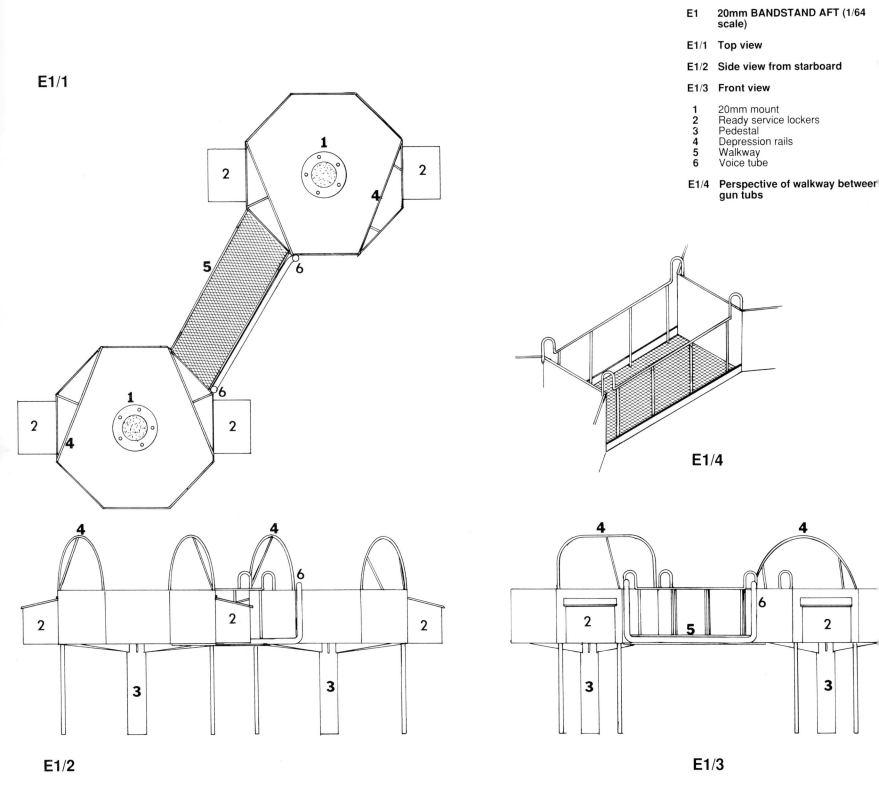

E1/1

E1/2

E1/3

E1/4

E1   **20mm BANDSTAND AFT (1/64 scale)**

E1/1   **Top view**

E1/2   **Side view from starboard**

E1/3   **Front view**

1   20mm mount
2   Ready service lockers
3   Pedestal
4   Depression rails
5   Walkway
6   Voice tube

E1/4   **Perspective of walkway between gun tubs**

AFT DECKHOUSE as in 1940 (1/64 scale)   **E2/1**

Top view

Side view – port

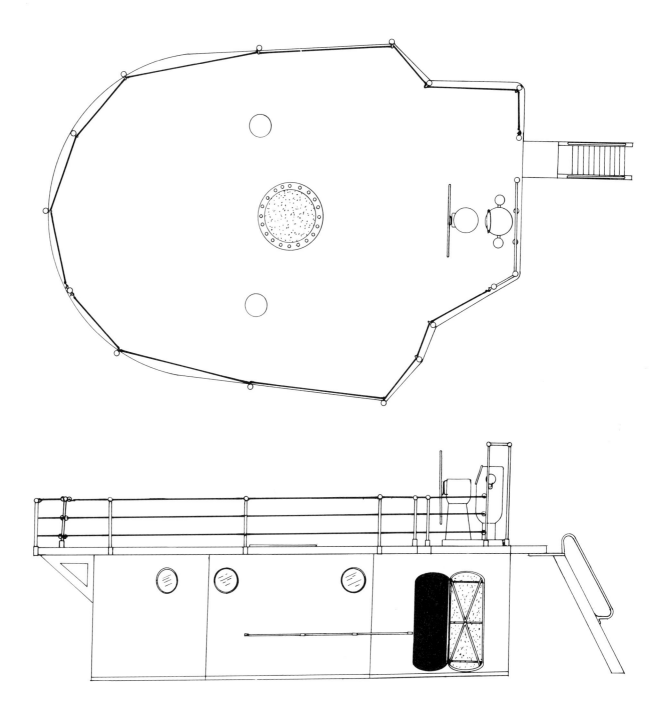

E2/2

E Superstructure

E2/3

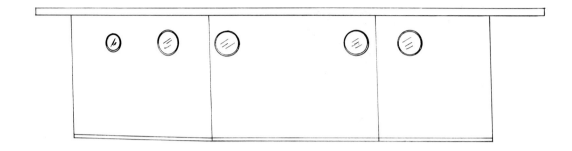

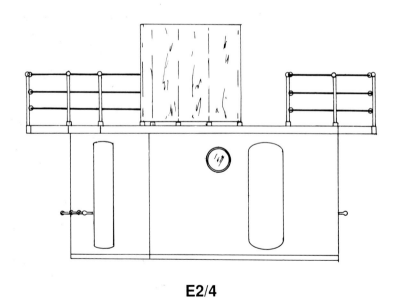

E2/4

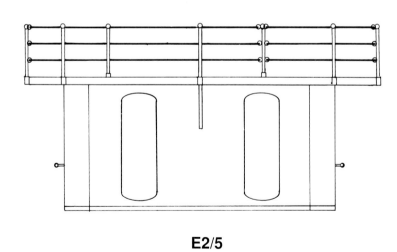

E2/5

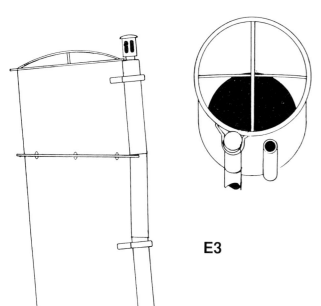

E3

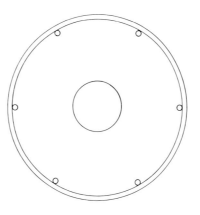

E3   NUMBER 3 STACK (typical; 1/64 scale)

E4   MIDSHIPS SEARCHLIGHT TOWER (1/64 scale)

E4

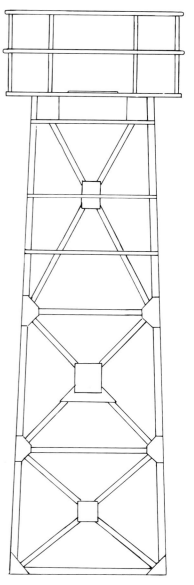

F Rig

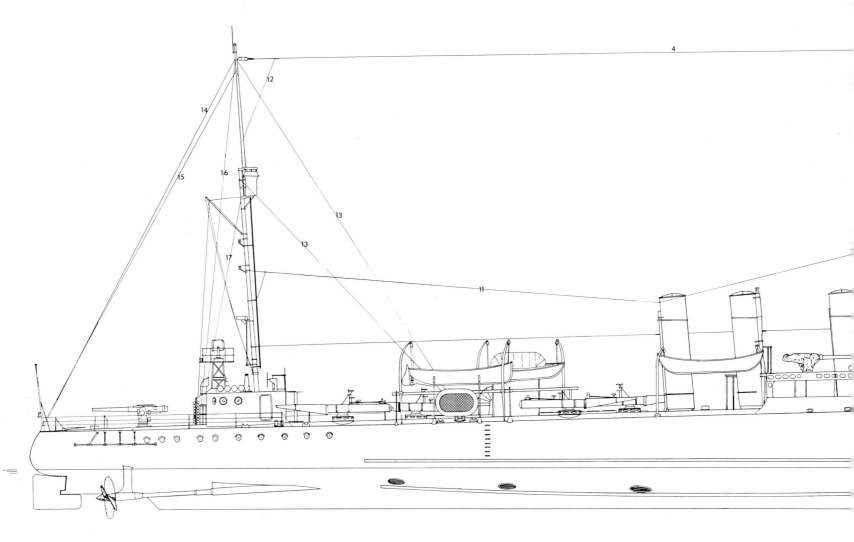

F1 **ANTENNA ARRANGEMENT as in 1919 (1/256 scale)**

1   Forestay – ½in galvanized steel wire rope
2   Dressing line – 2in tarred hemp
3   Lower forestay – ½in galvanized steel wire rope
4   Wireless antenna – No 7 silicon bronze
5   Manila guy line
6   Antenna lead in
7   Forward auxiliary antenna
8   Stay – ⅝in galvanzied steel wire rope
9   Whistle rope
10 Auxiliary antenna lead in
11 Aft auxiliary antenna
12 Guy line
13 Stay – ⅝in galvanized steel wire rope
14 Stay – ½in galvanized steel wire rope
15 Dressing line – 2in tarred hemp
16 Stay – ⁷⁄₁₆in galvanized steel wire rope
17 Stay – ⅝in galvanized steel wire rope

F1

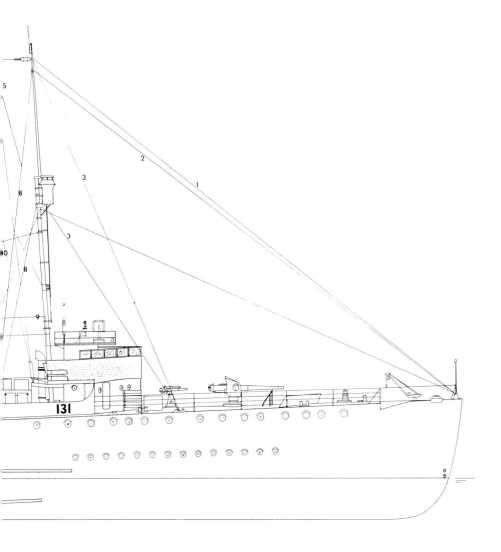

F2   **CROW'S NEST (1/24 scale)**

1   Shell
2   Weather shield
3   Topmast
4   Mast
5   Brace
6   Ladder

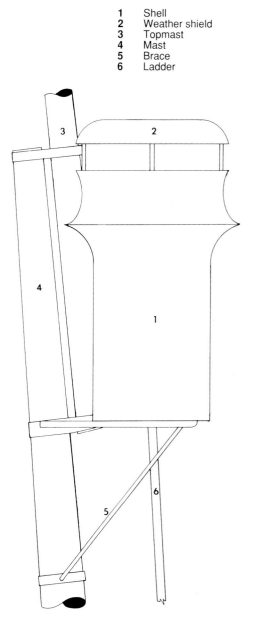

F2

G Armament

1 Barrel
2 Pointer's scope
3 Trunnion
4 Elevating handwheel
5 Elevating drive gear
6 Seat bracket
7 Recoil cylinder
8 Seat
9 Recoil cylinder
10 Saddle
11 Breech
12 Stand
13 Sight mount
14 Trainer's sight
15 Sight yoke
16 Trainer's handwheel
17 Smith-Astbury operating gear
18 Training gear
19 Elevating gear

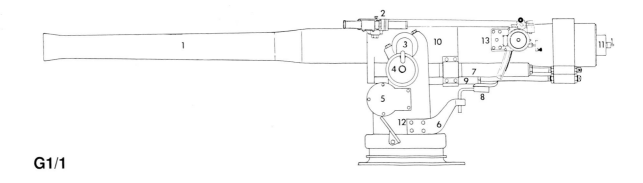

G1/1

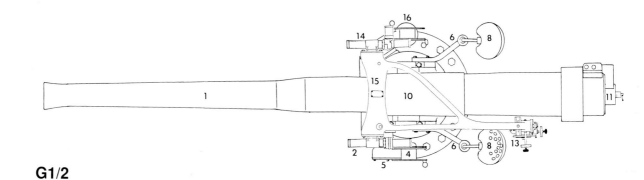

G1/2

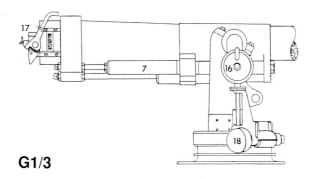

G1/3

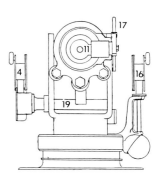

G

Shield for forward mount

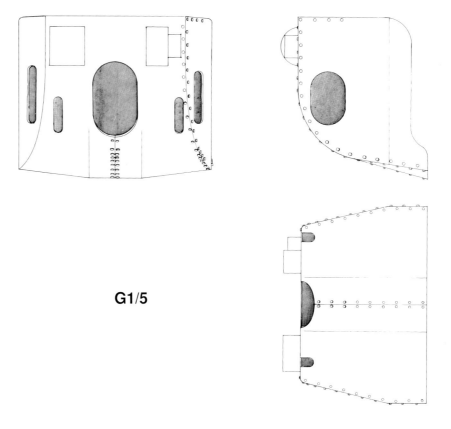

G1/5

Yoke sight (no scale)

Pointer's scope
Trainer's scope
Scope mount
Main yoke
Azimuth gear handwheel
Range dial
Sight bar and head
Elevating gear
Mounting bracket
Elevating arc

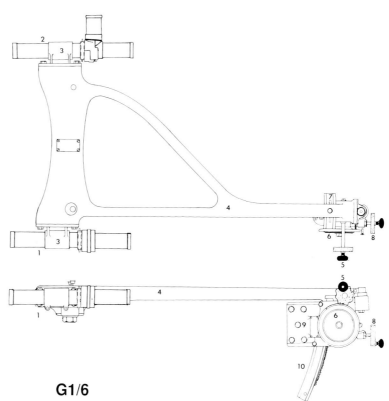

G1/6

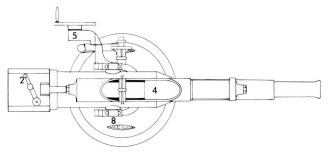

G2/2

G2   3in/23.5 Mk 14 (1/24 scale)

G2/1 Side view

G2/2 Top view

G2/3 Front view

1   Sliding breech
2   Breech operating mechanism
3   Elevating arc
4   Recoil cylinder
5   Elevating gear
6   Head lock
7   Stand
8   Trunnion

G3   12pdr/12cwt GUN ON HA/LA MOUNTING (All drawings by Lambert)

G3/1 Lefthand elevation (1/24 scale)

G3/2 Front of shield (1/24 scale)

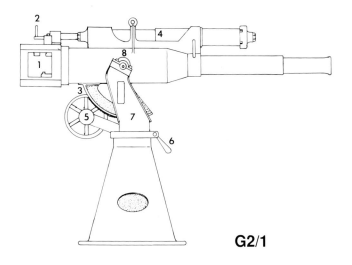

G2/1

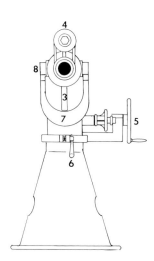

G2/3

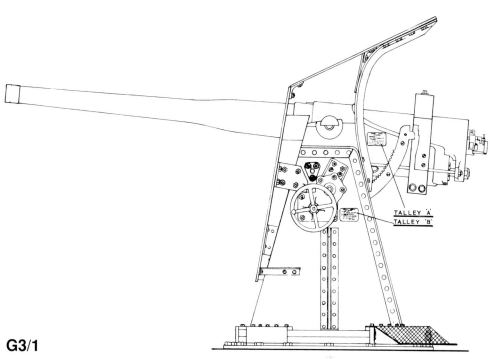

G3/1

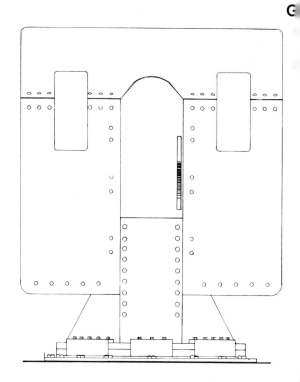

G3/3

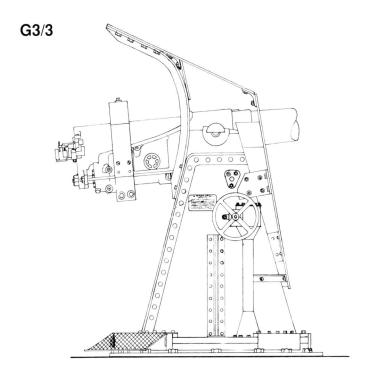

G3/4

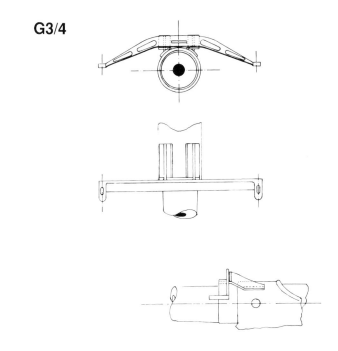

Righthand elevation (1/24 scale)

Detail of sight bed on cradle (1/24 scale)

General view, minus shield (no scale)

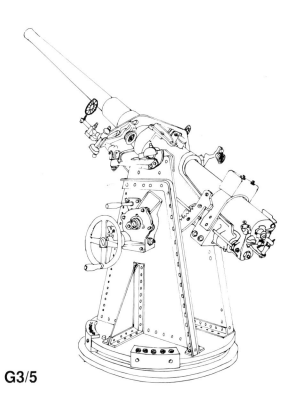

G3/5

G Armament

G3/6 Barrel and cradle, lefthand side
(1/24 scale)

G3/7 Barrel and cardle, righthand side
(1/24 scale)

G3/8 Enlarged view of breech end (no
scale)

G3/9 Enlarged section of recoil cylinder
and run-out springs (no scale)

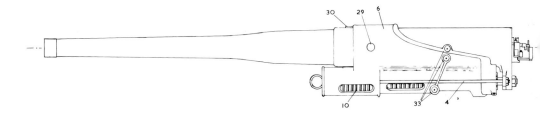

G3/6

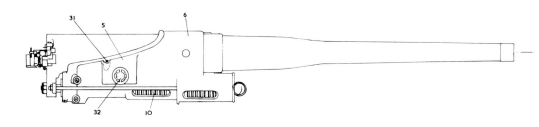

G3/7

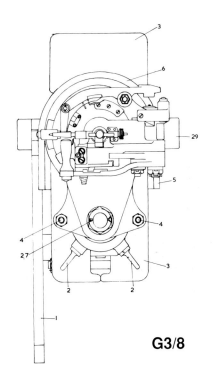

G3/8

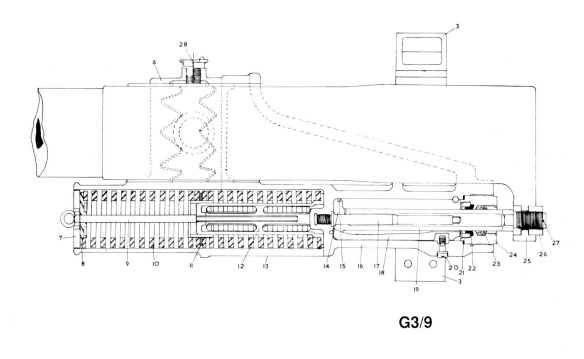

G3/9

G3/10 Enlarged front view of gun (no scale)

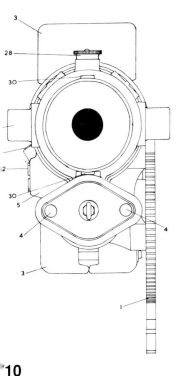

10

Elevating arc
Eyebolts for secring chains
Balance weight (HA/LA Mk IX mounting only)
Run out rods
Filling tank
Cradle
Crosshead
Compressor plate
Compression rod
Springs
Distance piece
Spring compressor
Run-out spring casing
Piston head
Manganese bronze ring
Recoil cylinder
Controlling plunger
Valve key
Piston rod
Screw securing valve key
Leather washer
'Hat' leather washer
Cotton packing
Cylinder closing plug
Lug
Securing nut
Keep pin
Oil
Trunnions
Gun keys
Filling plug
Cleaning plug
Lugs for elevating arc

G3/11 Breech mechanism, Mk IA and Mk IIA guns (no scale)

1 Catch retaining cartridge
2 Spring and plunger
3 Breech screw
4 Radial fixing screw
5 Trigger head
6 Volute spring
7 Catch retaining BM (breech mechanism) lever closed
8 Safety top
9 Carrier
10 Cocking cam
11 Link actuating breech screw
12 Cam groove
13 BM lever
14 Striker head
15 Recocking handle
16 Stop bracket
17 Nut retaining striker
18 Catch retaining carrier open
19 Cam
20 Carrier hinge pin
21 Extractor
22 Indicating marks

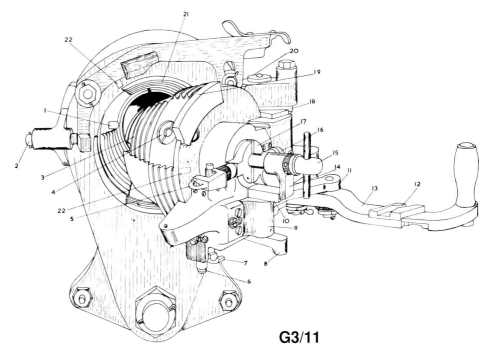

G3/11

97

G Armament

G3/12

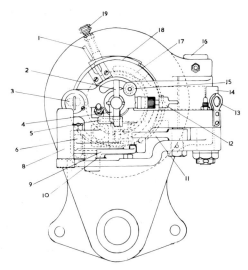

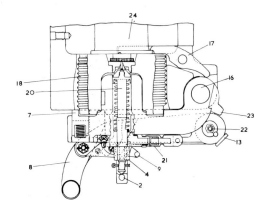

G3/12 Breech mechanism, Mk V gun, lanyard firing (no scale)

G3/13 Breech mechanism, Mk I, II and II* guns (no scale)

1	Safety marks	26	Stud
2	Recocking handle	27	Volute spring
3	Catch retaining breech screw open	28	Safety cam
4	Striker head	29	Sliding block
5	Cocking cam	30	Nut retaining striker
6	Catch retaining BM (breech mechanism) lever closed	31	Radial fixing screw
7	Catch retaining BM lever open	32	Spring
8	BM lever	33	Buffer
9	Safety stop	34	Eccentric groove
10	Cam groove	35	Actuating plate
11	Link actuating breech screw	36	Axis pin
12	Trigger head	37	Extractor lever
13	Lanyard guide	38	Retaining nut
14	Carrier	39	Fixing screw
15	Stop bracket	40	Loop for firing lanyard
16	Carrier hinge pin	41	Trigger
17	Extractor	42	Sear
18	Breech screw	43	Cock notch
19	Catch retaining cartridge	44	Main spring
20	Striker	45	Firing pin
21	Trigger retaining cap	46	Set screw
22	BM lever axis	47	Stop bracket
23	Cam actuating extractor	48	Striker head
24	Cartridge	49	Spindle
25	Metal bush	50	Carrier arm

G3/14 Breech (closed) and extractor, Mk I, I*, II and II* guns (no scale)

G3/15 Gunlayer's sight (no scale)

G3/14

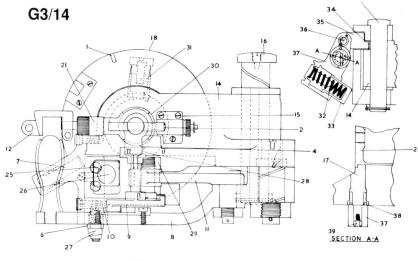

SECTION A-A

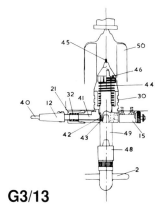

G3/13

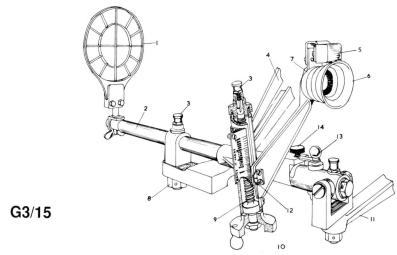

G3/15

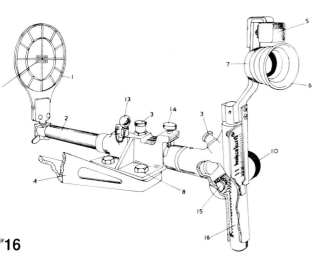

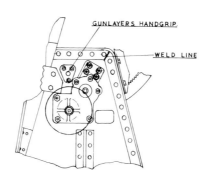

16

G3/17

GUNLAYERS HANDGRIP

WELD LINE

G3/16 Trainer's sight (no scale)

1 Foresight
2 Sight arm
3 Oil
4 Sight bracket
5 Rubber headrest
6 Rubber eyepiece
7 Backsight
8 Adustment for line
9 Range screw
10 Range handwheel
11 Bracket attached to trunnion
12 Range index pointer
13 Securing pin
14 Housing screw
15 Range pinion
16 Range rack
17 Deflection graduation for LA firing

G3/17 Detail of elevating gear (no scale)

G3/18 Detail of mounting base (1/24 scale)

G3/19 Elevating gear Mk IX mounting (no scale)

1 Bevel pinions
2 Worm
3 Spring and oil buffer
4 Elevation limit stop
5 Securing bolts to cradle
6 Elevating arc
7 Elevating pinions
8 Friction washers
9 Wormwheel
10 Oil
11 Gunlayer's handgrip
12 Belleville spring washer
13 Elevating handwheel
14 Elevating housing top

G3/20 Detail of cradle retaining breech screw open (no scale)

1 Spring
2 Carrier
3 Breech screw
4 Catch retaining breech screw open

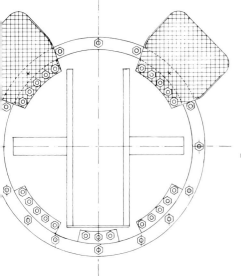

18

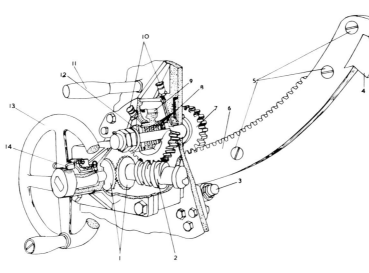

G3/19

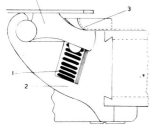

G3/20

G4/1

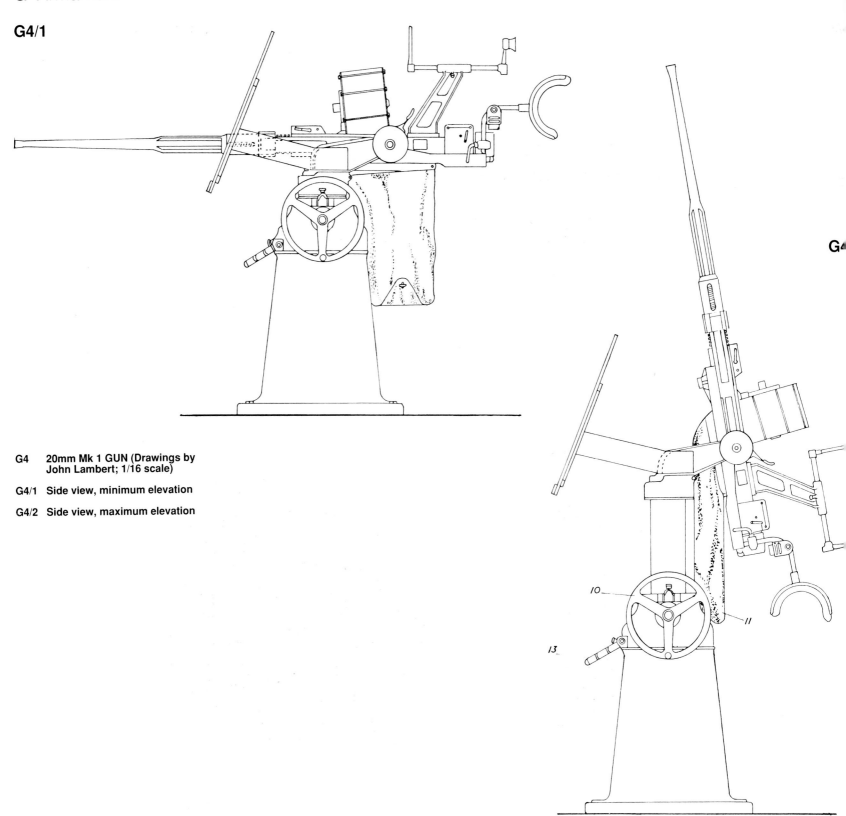

G4 20mm Mk 1 GUN (Drawings by John Lambert; 1/16 scale)

G4/1 Side view, minimum elevation

G4/2 Side view, maximum elevation

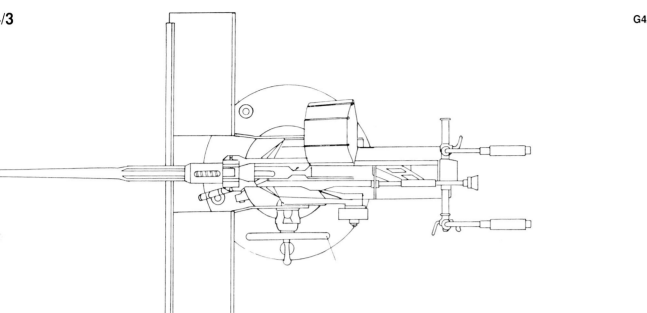

G4/4 Magazine (no scale)

1	Cover plate
2	Front plate
3	Mouth piece
4	Cartridge feeder
5	Spring loaded plunger
6	Roller
7	Feed head
8	Rollers
9	Feed links
10	Articulating bolts
11	Feed arm
12	Feed block
13	Drum
14	Spiral path
15	Spring casing
16	Clock spring
17	Spiral groove
18	Indicator block
19	Spring axis
20	Feed axis
21	Cross pin
22	Coupling sleeve
23	Coupling spring
24	Coupling retaining ring

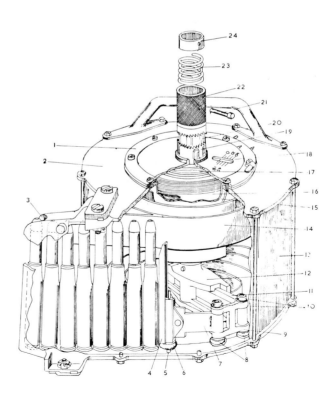

G4/4

G Armament

G4/5 Gun detail, side view

G4/6 Gun detail, top view

1   Cooling vanes
2   Barrel spring casing
3   Barrel springs
4   Buffer
5   Breech bar
6   Magazine catch lever
7   Magazine
8   Sight
9   Range setting wheel
10   Shoulder rest
11   Hand grip
12   Trigger
13   Double loading stop
14   Cocking stud for lanyard
15   Barrel locking lever
16   Barrel locking handle
17   Safety catch
18   Cotter
19   Safety harness
20   Pedestal
21   Cartridge case collecting bag
22   Clamping screw

G4/5

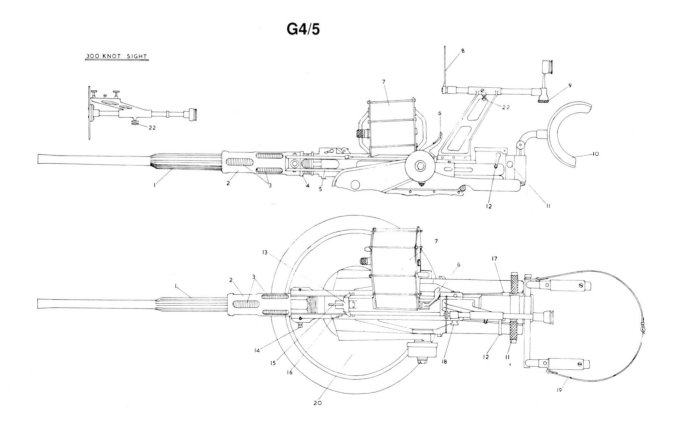

G4/6

G5/1

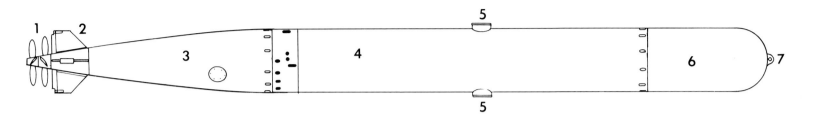

G5 **Mk 8 TORPEDO**

G5/1 General arrangement (1/32 scale)

1 Contra-rotating propellers
2 Fins
3 Afterbody
4 Air flask
5 Guide studs
6 Warhead
7 Lifting eye

G5/2 Tail section (no scale)

1 Elevator
2 Fin
3 Rudder
4 Hinge
5 Contra-rotating propellers
6 Exhaust

G5/3 Warhead (no scale)

1 Exploder
2 Cast TNT
3 Stiffeners
4 Bulkhead

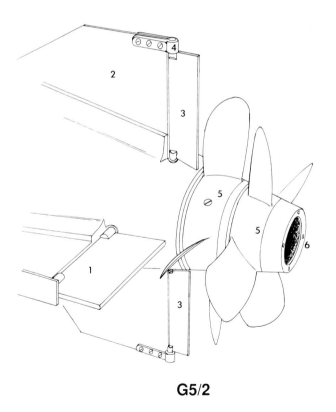

G5/2

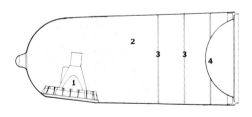

G5/3

G Armament

G6   **TORPEDO TUBES (1/32 scale)**

G6/1 **Side view**

G6/2 **Top view**

1   Breech door
2   Impulse chamber
3   Barrel
4   Saddle
5   Stand
6   Spoon
7   Spoon extension
8   Hinge
9   Trainer's seat
10   Training handwheel
11   Training sight

G6/1

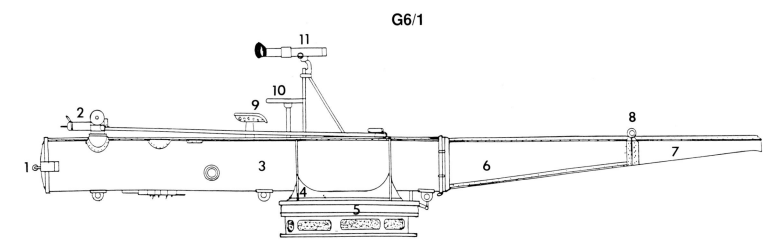

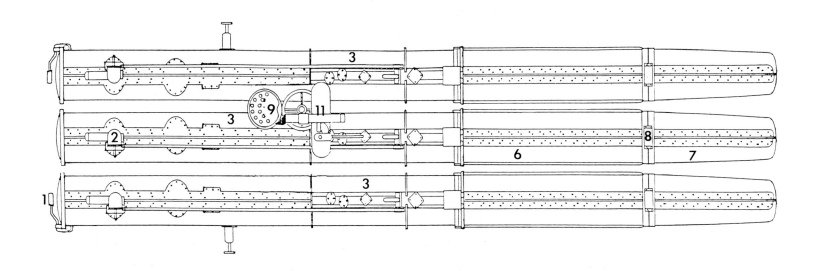

G6/2

/1

G7	**DEPTH CHARGE Mk 3 (1/16 scale)**
G7/1	**Side view**
G7/2	**End view**
G7/3	**Section**

1	Casing
2	Booster extender
3	Booster
4	Pistol and detonator
5	Safety fork
6	Cast TNT
7	Inlet valve

G8	**DEPTH CHARGE TRACK (1/32 scale)**
G8/1	**Top view**
G8/2	**Side view**

1	Main frame
2	Extension to clear hull
3	Forward detent
4	Side rail
5	Aft detent

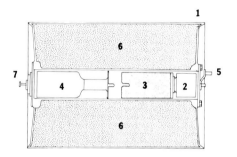

G7/3

G8/1

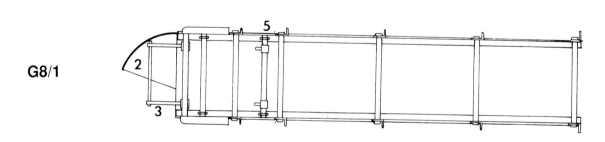

G8/2

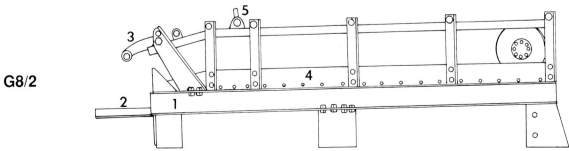

105

G Armament

G9 **DEPTH CHARGE DAVIT (no scale)**

G9/1 **Side view**

G9/2 **Details of fittings**

G9/3 **Davit head**

G10 **DEPTH CHARGE PROJECTOR Mk IV (no scale; drawing by John Lambert)**

1 Wire strop
2 Tumbler hook
3 Depth charge tray
4 Surge tank
5 Pipe to arrestor cylinder
6 Exhaust ports
7 Carrier piston
8 Barrel

G9/1   **G9/2**   **G9/3**

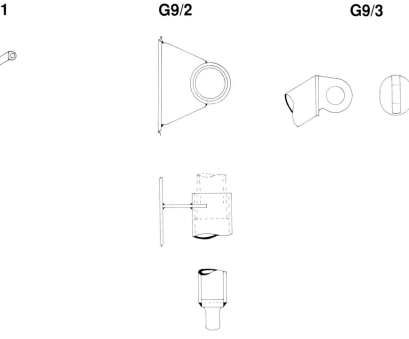

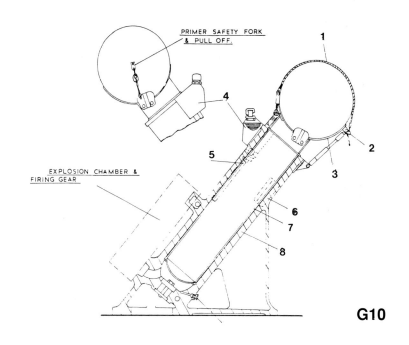

PRIMER SAFETY FORK & PULL OFF.

EXPLOSION CHAMBER & FIRING GEAR

G10

Fire control

DOTTER DIRECTORSCOPE

TORPEDO DIRECTOR (no scale)

Scope
Bearing indicator scale
Hand grip
Training gear
Stand

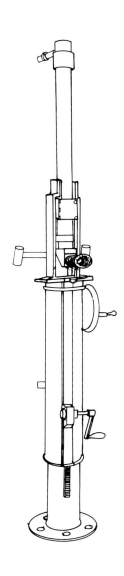

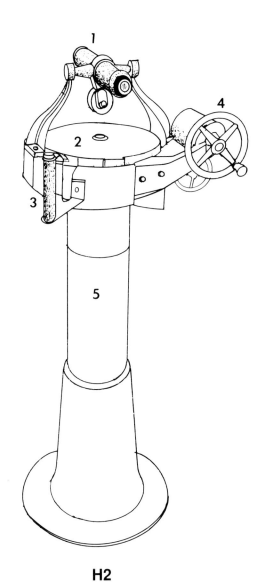

H1

H2

I Fittings

I1/1

I2

I1/2

I1/3

I3/1

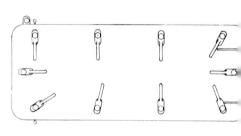

I3/2

I3/3

I4

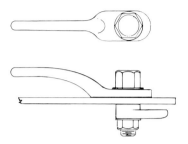

I4   HATCH DOG (no scale)

I5   HAWSE REEL (1/48 scale)

I6   Aft 4in AMMUNITION SCUTTLE
(1/24 scale)

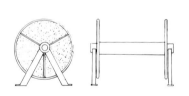 

I5

I6

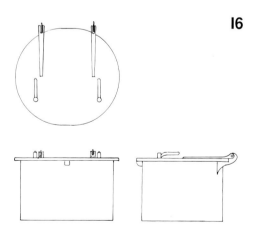

I Fittings

I7 **FORWARD MAIN ENGINE ROOM HATCH (1/32 scale)**

I8 **AFT MAIN ENGINE ROOM HATCH**

I8/1 Top view (1/32 scale)

I8/2 Isolated hatch view (no scale)

I8/3 End view (1/32 scale)

I7

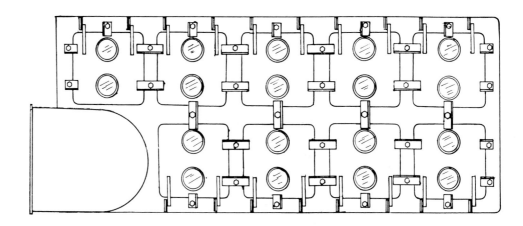

I8/1

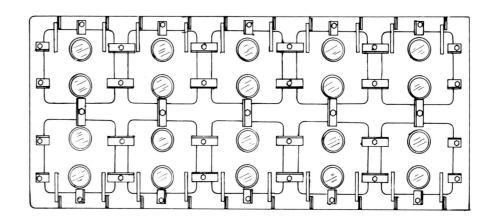

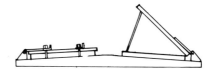

I8/2

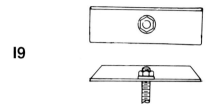

I9

I9　**MAIN ENGINE ROOM HATCH DOG**
(no scale)

I10　**ENGINE ROOM VENT (1/32 scale)**

I10/1　Top view

I10/2　Side view

I10/3　Front view

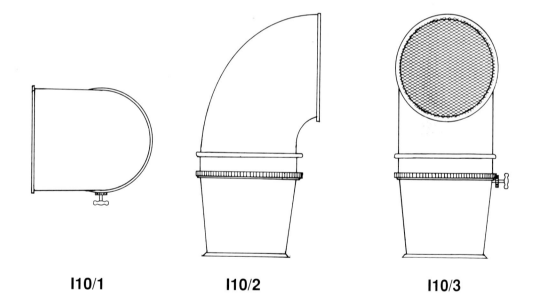

I10/1　　　　　**I10/2**　　　　　**I10/3**

I Fittings

I11   ACCOMMODATION LADDER (no scale)

I11/1   Top view

I11/2   Side view

1   Platform
2   Ladder
3   Landing platform
4   Ladder support stanchion

I12   INCLINED LADDER (no scale)

I12/1   Side view

I12/2   Front view

1   Railing
2   Ladder
3   Stanchion

I12/3   Ladder details

1   Tread
2   Side frame
3   Clip

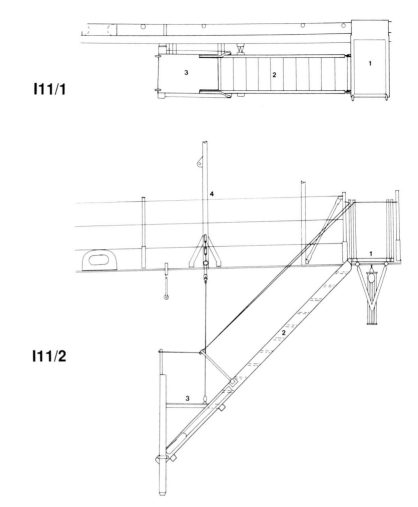

I11/1

I11/2

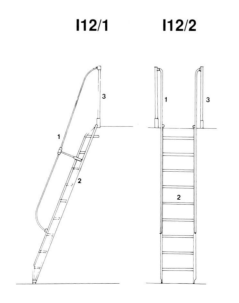

I12/1   **I12/2**   **I12/3**

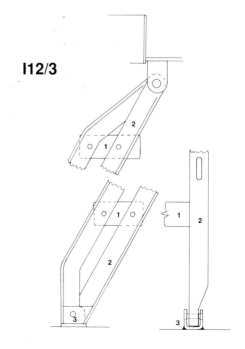

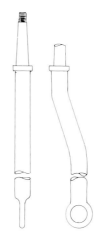

I14

I13

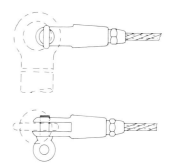

I15

J Ground tackle

J1   **STOCK TYPE ANCHOR (1/24 scale)**

J2   **ANCHOR DAVIT (1/64 scale)**

J1

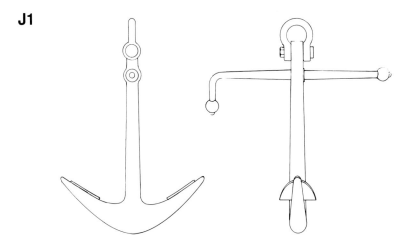

J2

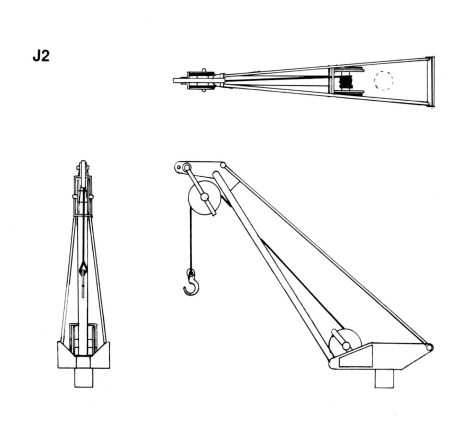

J3 DETACHABLE LINK (assembled and unassembled)

1 Lead ball
2 Forelock pin
3 Forelock
4 Link body

J4 CAPSTAN (1/24 scale)

J5 CHAIN PIPES (1/24 scale)

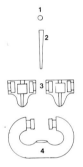

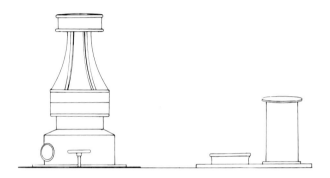

J4

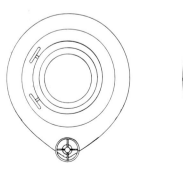

J5

K Boats

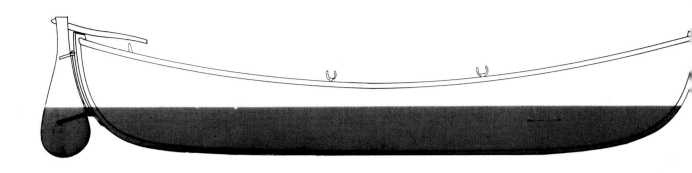

K1   **24ft WHALEBOAT (1/48 scale)**

K1/1   **General arrangement**

K1/2   **Inboard profile**

K1/1

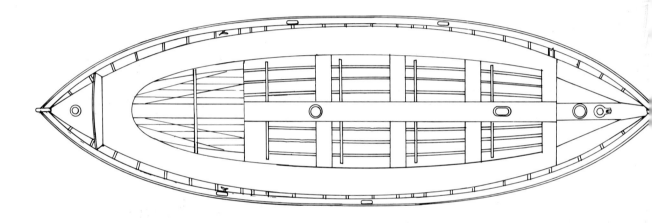

K1/2

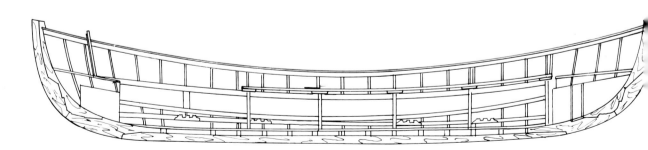

K1/3

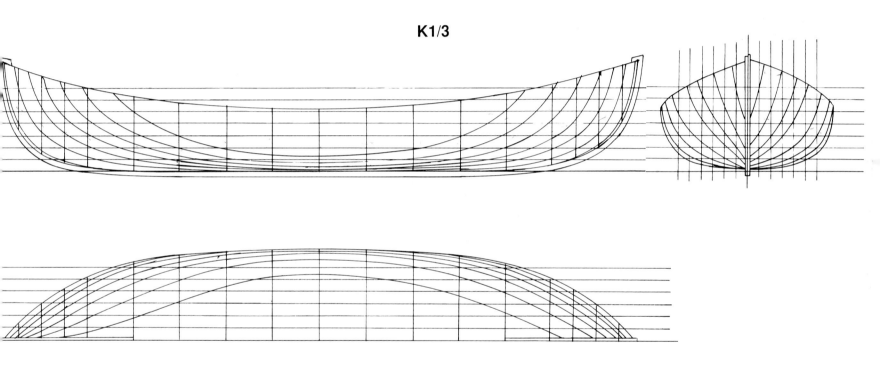

K Boats

K2   24ft MOTOR LAUNCH (1/48 scale)

K2/1 General arrangement

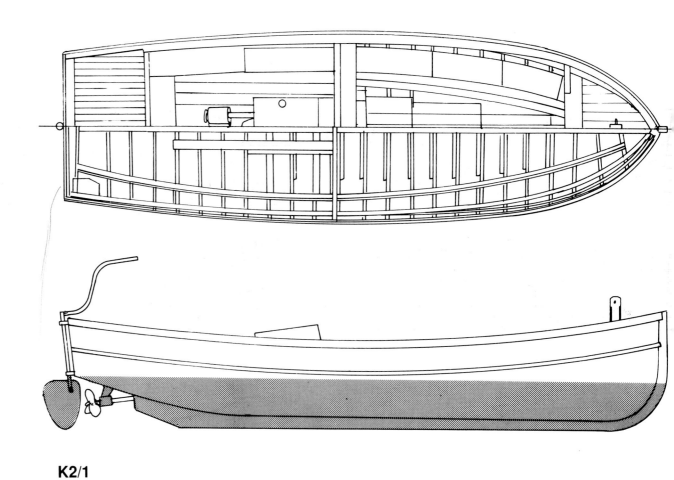

K2/1

K2/2

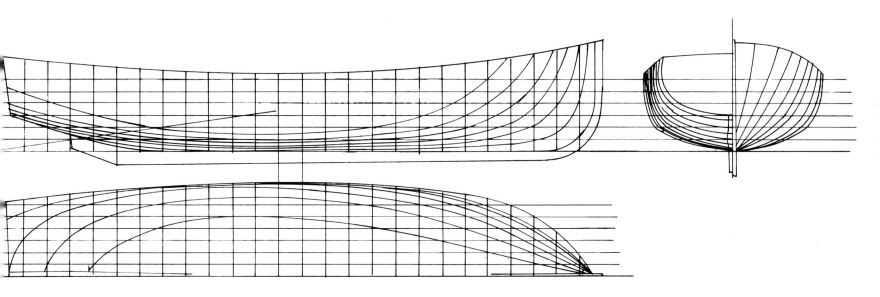

K3   26ft MOTOR WHALEBOAT (1/48 scale)

K3/1   General arrangement

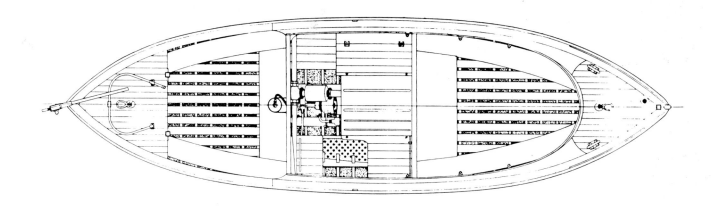

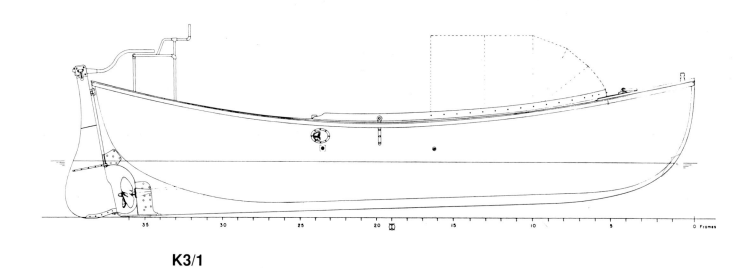

K3/1

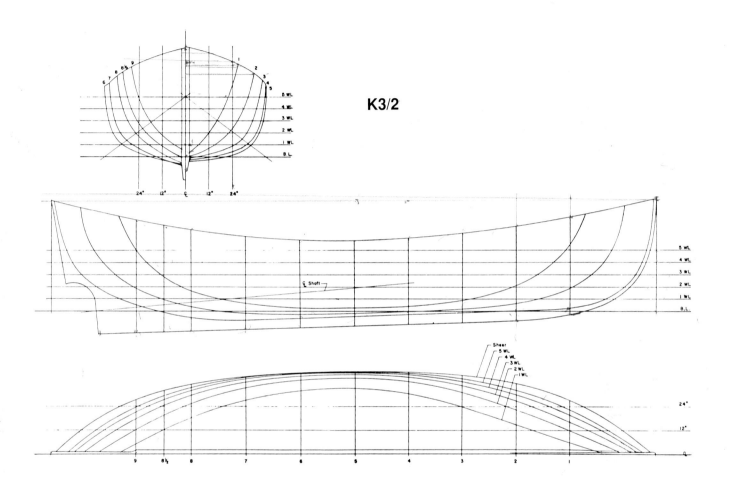

K3/2

K Boats

K3/3

K3/4

K3/5

K3/6

K3/7

K3/3 Frame 3 looking forward

K3/4 Frame 5 looking forward

K3/5 Frame 15 looking forward

K3/6 Frame 17 looking aft

K3/7 Frame 19 loking forward

K4/1

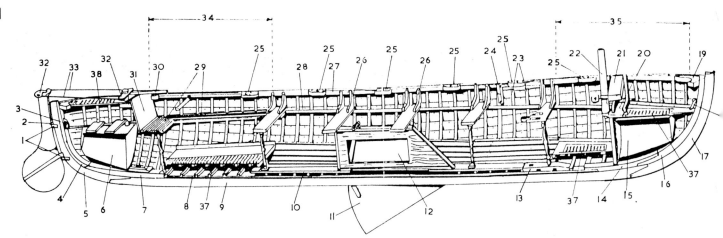

K4	27ft MOTOR WHALEBOAT (Drawings by John Lambert; 1/48 scale)	K4/4	Half-breadth plan	20	Towing thwart

K4/1 General arrangement	1	Gudgeons	21	Towing strongback
	2	Pintles	22	Towing bollard
K4/2 Outboard profile	3	Sternpost ringbolt	23	Timber
	4	After apron	24	Shroud plate
K4/3 Longitudinal section	5	Sternpost	25	Socket for crutch
	6	After bouyancy tank	26	Knee
	7	After deadwood	27	Gunwale
	8	Hog	28	Rising
	9	Keel	29	Stern benches
	10	Keelson	30	Tiller
	11	Centreboard	31	Blackboard
	12	Keel box	32	Yokes
	13	Mast step	33	Yoke lines
	14	Fore deadwood	34	Stern sheets
	15	Fore buoyancy tank	35	Head sheets
	15	Fore apron	36	Bilge rail with handholes
	16	Stem	37	Grating
	18	Stem ringbolt	73	Lifelines
	19	Breast hook	74	Ship's crest

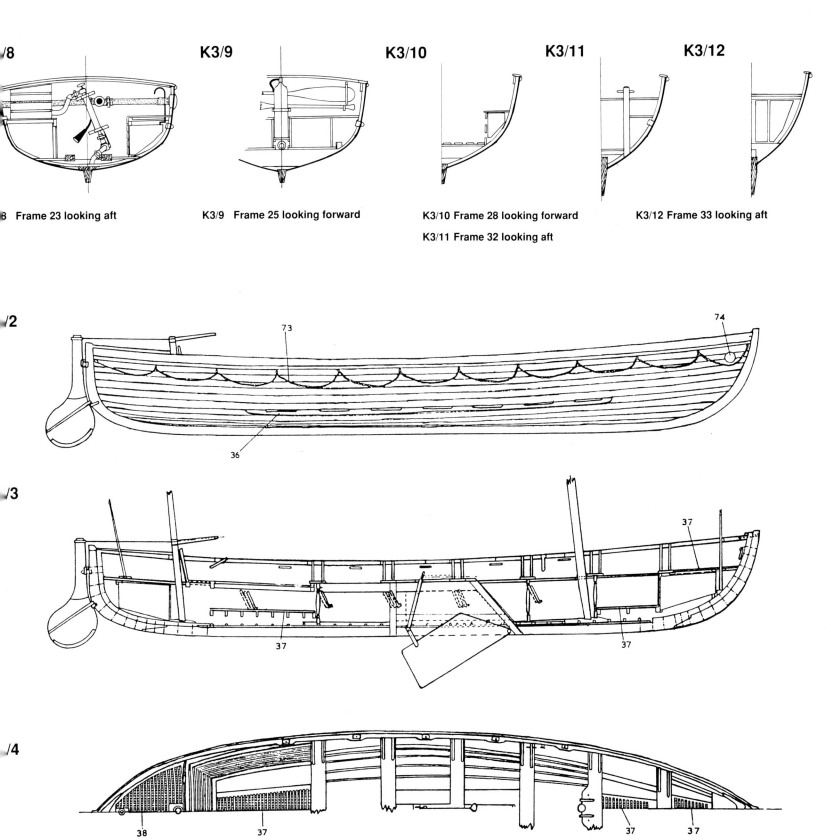

K3/8

K3/9

K3/10

K3/11

K3/12

8 Frame 23 looking aft

K3/9 Frame 25 looking forward

K3/10 Frame 28 looking forward

K3/11 Frame 32 looking aft

K3/12 Frame 33 looking aft

/2

/3

/4

K Boats

K5   BOAT SKIDS (1/64 scale)

K5/1   Top view

K5/2   Side view

K5/3   Cross-section showing lightened
I-beam construction

K5/1

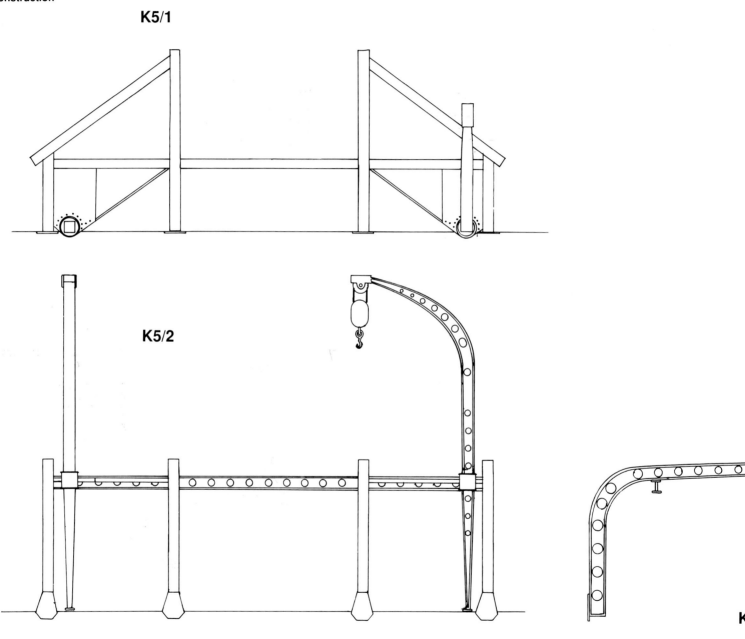

K5/2

K5

K6

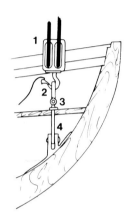

K6   LIFTING ARRANGEMENT (no scale)

1   Double block
2   Raymond releasing hook
3   Lifting eye
4   Lifting eye support

K7

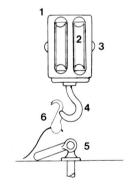

K7   RAYMOND RELEASING HOOK (no scale)

1   Block body
2   Sheave
3   Sheave pin
4   Main hook
5   Lifting eye
6   Safety hook

L Camouflage

L1   WESTERN APPROACHES
       SCHEME (carried by Campbeltown
       in 1941; based on photos of other
       Towns in this scheme, it would
       appear that the starboard side was
       identical; 1/256 scale)

L1

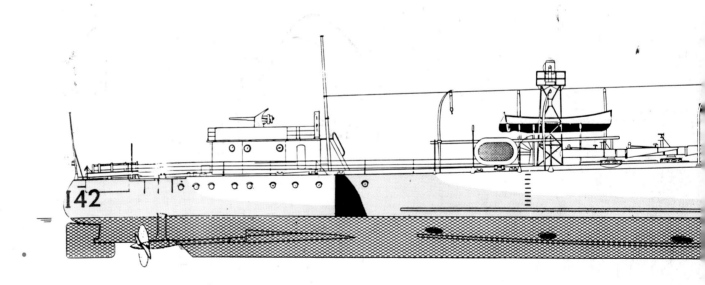

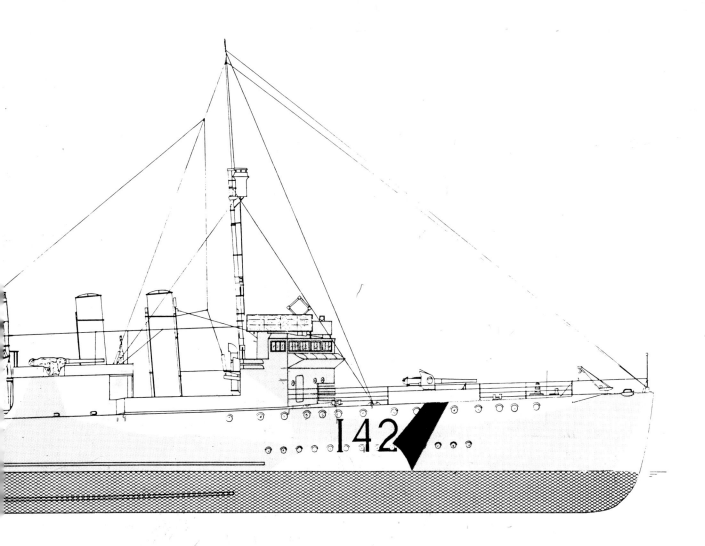